GIVING
THE BLESSING

Gary Smalley
and John Trent, Ph.D.

A
JANET
THOMA
BOOK

THOMAS NELSON PUBLISHERS
Nashville

Published in Nashville, Tennessee, by Thomas Nelson, Inc.

Scripture quotations are from the NEW KING JAMES VERSION of the Bible. Copyright © 1979, 1980, 1982, Thomas Nelson, Inc., Publishers.

Scripture quotations taken from the HOLY BIBLE: NEW INTERNATIONAL VERSION® are marked (NIV) in the text. Copyright © 1973, 1978, 1984 by International Bible Society. Used by permission of Zondervan Publishing House. All rights reserved.

Scripture quotations taken from the REVISED STANDARD VERSION of the Bible are marked (RSV) in the text. Copyright © 1946, 1952, 1971, 1973 by the Division of Christian Education of the National Council of the Churches of Christ in the U.S.A. Used by permission.

Scripture quotations taken from THE NEW AMERICAN STANDARD BIBLE are marked throughout (NASB). Copyright © 1960, 1962, 1963, 1968, 1971, 1972, 1973, 1975, 1977 by The Lockman Foundation and are used by permission.

Library of Congress Cataloging-in-Publicata Data

Smalley, Gary.
    Giving the blessing / by Gary Smalley, John Trent
      p.   cm.
    ISBN 0-8407-4557-5
    1. Benediction. 2. Family—Religious life. I. Trent, John T.
II. Title.
BV197.B5S55   1993   249—dc20   92–40627
                                      CIP

Printed in the United States of America
5 6 — 98

To Dave:

May the Lord bless you with "His" blessing & may you always be able to give

GIVING
THE BLESSING

"His" blessing to others.

Love
Jayne

1-16-99
John Trents Seminar at
the 1st Baptist church

I will bless you . . . and you shall be a blessing.
—GEN. 12:2

Every child longs for it. Every friend can use it. Every marriage partner needs it. And you have the power to give it—each day of the year.

We're talking about the ancient practice of expressing affirmation and commitment to others by extending a blessing to them. Blessing others was an essential part of Old Testament family life. This has also become a meaningful part of our own lives. And we believe it can be an incredible source of richness and joy for you as well.

We believe you want to be a source of support and reassurance to those around you. This daily devotional guide can help by providing insight, encouragement, and practical ideas. In a sense, it is a mini-workbook to help you weave blessing into the fabric of your everyday life. In the process, we hope it helps you gain a richer sense of being blessed by God and others.

Let us begin, then, with a blessing for you:

May God's richest blessings be upon you both today and throughout the year—and may those blessings flow through you to touch the lives of everyone you meet.

> *Then Melchizedek king of Salem brought out bread
> and wine; he was the priest of God Most High. And
> he blessed him.*
> —GEN. 14:18–19

Exactly what do we mean by *the blessing*? The first definition of the English word *bless* means "to consecrate or make holy." It also means "to invoke divine care for," "to speak of gratefully," and "to confer prosperity or happiness upon." Our use of the word encompasses all those meanings. But we also mean something much more specific when we talk of the blessing. We refer to the age-old practice of building relationships and self-worth by expressing affirmation and a sense of responsibility to others.

This practice has deep biblical roots. In the Old Testament, the Hebrew word translated *bless* "to bow the knee." In other words, to give "honor" to others. It describes God's actions toward people (". . . I will bless you . . . ." Gen. 12:2) and people's actions toward God ("Bless the LORD, O my soul . . . ." Ps. 103:1). But it also describes a deliberate practice of expressing honor and devotion to other people, as in today's Scripture. In this devotional book, over the course of the year, we will focus on the value of this third, relational act of blessing. We will discuss how we can make it part of our lives.

---

*What do you hope to gain through this year of studying the blessing?
Sum up your dreams and expectations in a sentence or two and keep
what you have written for future reference.*

*The blessing of the LORD be upon you; we bless you
in the name of the LORD!*
                                                —PS. 129:8

The blessing begins at home, in the parent-child relationship. Children who receive the gift of the blessing from their parents have a spiritual and emotional head start in life. They receive a sturdy foundation of love and acceptance. Because of this, many of the devotionals in this book will deal with blessing children.

However, studying the blessing in Scriptures, we have found its principles can be used in any intimate relationship. Husbands and wives can apply these principles to bless each other. Friendships can be deepened and strengthened. Church families can bring warmth, healing, and hope to brothers and sisters in Christ, many of whom never received an earthly blessing from their parents.

In fact, the ingredients of the blessing we give each other are the very relationship components God uses to bless His children—every one of us.

Pray that the blessing will begin in your home, then reach out to warm and transform all the relationships in your life.

> [Peter] said to [Jesus], "Yes, Lord; You know that I
> love You." He said to him, "Feed My lambs."
> —JOHN 21:15

Every person longs to be accepted. Some may say, "I don't care what other people think about me." But on the inside, everyone yearns for intimacy and affection.

In other words, we all enter this world hungry for a blessing. Sadly, many people go through their whole lives without ever having that hunger satisfied. As a result, children grow into insecure and unhappy adults—unable to break free from their parents. They are hampered in developing intimate relationships, hard-pressed to give praise or support to others.

The good news is: It doesn't have to be that way. God doesn't create a hunger without creating a source of satisfaction. He is the one who "fills the hungry soul with goodness" (Ps. 107:9). And in telling us to "feed My lambs," He calls us to help provide spiritual food for all those around us who are starving for a blessing.

Make a list of people in your life who may be hungry for a blessing. Start with your family, then list friends, co-workers, people in your church, and others. Don't forget to include yourself! God also offers nourishment for your "hungry soul."

"May God Almighty . . . give you the blessing of Abraham."
—GEN. 28:3–4

The tradition of blessing children is a very ancient practice. In fact, this ritual was probably familiar to Abraham even before God called him from Ur of the Chaldees. But with God's promise to Abraham and the unfolding of His redemptive work, the blessing began to hold special meaning to God's people.

For sons or daughters in biblical times, receiving the blessing was a momentous event. At a specific point in their lives they would hear their parents pronounce words of encouragement, love, and acceptance. They would hear their names linked with God's special promises and the special history of their people. What an occasion to anticipate!

Some aspects of this Old Testament blessing were unique to that era. However, the relationship elements of this blessing still apply today. We can daily build these elements of blessing into the lives of the people we love.

———————

Can you think of a specific time in your life when your father, mother, or another significant adult spoke a blessing to you? If so, what did that blessing mean in your life?

> *And he came near and kissed him; and he smelled*
> *the smell of his clothing, and blessed him and said:*
> *"Surely, the smell of my son is like the smell of a*
> *field which the LORD has blessed. Therefore may*
> *God give you of the dew of heaven, of the fatness of*
> *the earth, and plenty of grain and wine. Let*
> *peoples serve you, and nations bow down to you.*
> *Be master over your brethren, and let your mother's*
> *sons bow down to you. Cursed be everyone who*
> *curses you, and blessed be those who bless you!"*
> —GEN. 27:27–29

This Old Testament blessing, bestowed by Isaac upon his son Jacob, contains all the elements that make the blessing so powerful in a relationship. Eventually, we will explore these elements in detail. But for now, meditate on Isaac's words. Consider all the benefits they imply for Jacob.

What do you think Isaac was telling his son in this blessing? How would you convey the same message in contemporary language?

For the LORD your god has blessed you.
—DEUT. 2:7

The blessing is essentially an outward act which communicates love and esteem to other people. But like all forms of healthy communication, the act of blessing begins inside. Ideally, it begins with a sense of being blessed by God and others. Once we are secure in our own blessing, it's easy to share with others. Today, focus on the blessings in your own life. Think of people, opportunities, experiences. Make a list of the blessings you have received and thank God for them.

You may find it difficult to "feel blessed" or to even think of blessings. If so, just write: "God loves me and sent His Son to redeem me," and "God has promised to bless me and to use me to bless others." Add any incidental blessings you can think of—even those as basic as "I am not sick today." When you pray, thank God for these blessings, claim His promises, and ask for His healing.

Thank God for the blessings He has given you and claim His promise to make you a blessing in others' lives. Ask God's help, healing, and joy for yourself and for those you love.

> *Blessed be the God and Father of our Lord Jesus Christ, who has blessed us with every spiritual blessing.*
> —EPH. 1:3

In a world awash with insecurity, we need biblical anchors to grasp. In their search for acceptance, so many people accept a cure far worse than the actual problem. Many try to find themselves through traumatic recreations of the past. Others lose themselves through hypnosis or a similar psychological technique. But these techniques seldom, if ever, offer lasting change.

On the other hand, God, His Word, and His principles offer a changeless blueprint to follow as we construct, or reconstruct, relationships. The Bible spells out the concept of the blessing and repeatedly models it. Through God's Word, we also learn the principles of unconditional love that make the blessing possible. And more important, through God's persistent and redeeming love, we can receive the blessing and extend it to others.

Praise God. He is the One from whom all blessings flow.

Behold, children are a heritage from the LORD.
—PS. 127:3

Today, as in centuries past, orthodox Jewish homes bestow a special family blessing on their children. This blessing, which is much like the patriarchal blessing Isaac bestowed upon Jacob, has been vital in providing a sense of acceptance for generations of children.

You don't need to be Jewish to value children and give them a blessing. You don't even have to be a parent. Although parents hold a responsibility to bless their children, anyone can change a child's life. They can give a child a blessing by caring enough to express acceptance, model commitment, and picture a special future. In giving children the blessing, we help insure that they will carry the heritage of love.

Do you know children who need a blessing from you? Besides your own children, consider their friends. Also remember children in your church, in your neighborhood, and the children of your friends.

> *Whoever receives this little child in My name*
> *receives Me.*
> —LUKE 9:48

The practice of blessing children gives them an advantage as they move into their future. It also brings them great joy now. Children love to be blessed!

My wife, Cynthia, and I (John) have learned this in our family. Since our children were tiny, we have awakened them with a special song of blessing, which begins:

> *Good morning, good morning, how are you today?*
> *The Lord bless you and keep you throughout the*
> *day.*

One night, four-year-old Kari eloquently testified to how much that blessing meant to her. She bounced off to bed exclaiming, "'Nite, Mom. 'Nite Dad. And don't forget to bless me in the morning!"

You don't have to bless your children via song, and it doesn't have to be in the morning. But as you remember to bless the little ones you love, you will reap great dividends of joy.

*Blessed shall you be when you come in, and
blessed shall you be when you go out.*

—DEUT. 28:6

D*on't let them out of your sight without a blessing.*
That's a key idea connected with the blessing of children in orthodox Jewish homes. That concept is based on the reality that a family blessing offers children (and others) a protective tool to help them survive in this dangerous world.

Remember, everyone is hungry for love, acceptance, and affirmation. And the world is full of counterfeit offers—drugs, illicit sex, cults. The best defense against a child's succumbing to imagined acceptance is to provide him or her with genuine acceptance. By giving a child genuine acceptance and affirmation at home, you can greatly reduce the likelihood that he or she will seek approval from a group of drug-using peers or in an immoral relationship.

You offer valuable protection for children in a dangerous world when you raise them in an atmosphere of blessing. Pray that God will grant you the loving perseverance to raise this protective shield in your home.

> *And all these blessings shall come upon you and*
> *overtake you, because you obey the voice of the*
> *LORD your God: "Blessed shall you be in the city,*
> *and blessed shall you be in the country. Blessed*
> *shall be the fruit of your body, the produce of your*
> *ground and the increase of your herds, the increase*
> *of your cattle and the offspring of your flocks."*
> —DEUT. 28:2–4

Blessings in the Old Testament were given to whole nations as well as to individuals. Today's Scripture was from a series of blessings pronounced upon the children of Israel as they prepared to enter Canaan. Blessings were also exchanged between God and His people.

An important result of this pattern of blessing was the strengthening of bonds—between family members, among individuals in a group, and between God and His people. That is also one important purpose of the blessing today. Giving and receiving the blessing reinforces relationships by repeating words of love, respect, and commitment.

Which of your relationships do you value most? Pray that God will strengthen these bonds of love as you become more skilled and determined at blessing others.

*Therefore a man shall leave his father and his
mother and shall become united and cleave to his
wife.*
—GEN. 2:24 NASB

Many books and tapes point out the need for husbands and wives to cleave to spouses. However, very few talk about the tremendous need for couples to "leave" home. Perhaps this is because people have often thought of leaving home as simply moving away physically. But leaving home has always meant more than putting physical distance between us and our parents. Leaving home carries not only the idea of physical separation, but also the thought of *emotional* separation.

Most people who have never acquired their parents' blessing find great emotional difficulty leaving home. Perhaps years have passed since they have seen their parents, but unmet needs for personal acceptance can emotionally chain them to their parents. As a result, a person in this situation is unable to genuinely cleave to another person in a lasting relationship. Before someone can defeat the problem and build a healthy relationship, he or she must first understand the concept of the blessing.

The blessing frees children to move forward and develop healthy adult relationships.

> *So [Simeon] came by the Spirit into the temple. And
> when the parents brought in the Child Jesus, to do
> for Him according to the custom of the law, he took
> Him up in his arms and blessed God.*
> —LUKE 2:27–28

From Old Testament times to today the blessing has been an important gift offered to Jewish children. In fact, giving the blessing to their children has been considered a *duty* for parents. Giving the blessing to children has also been a regular part of the rabbi's duties on *Shabbat* (the Sabbath), feast and holy days.

For instance, the *Brantshpiegal*, a book on Jewish family life and practices written in 1602, records these instructions: "Before the children can walk, they should be carried on the Sabbath and on the Holy Days to their father and mother to receive their blessing. After they are able to walk, they should go to them of their own accord, with body bent and with head bowed, to receive the Blessing."

What a wonderful way to raise secure, confident children—by beginning to bless the children from the time they are very tiny and continuing to bless them as they grow.

Even today, raising our children with the blessing is the most precious gift we can give them.

Consider the lilies of the field, how they grow.
—MATT. 6:28

A flower cannot grow without several necessary elements. Every flower needs soil, air, water, light, and a secure place to grow. When these five basic ingredients are present, you'll find it almost impossible to keep the flower from growing. The same is true when it comes to the basic elements of the blessing.

The blessing also has five key elements. Each individual part provides a unique, necessary contribution to giving the blessing. A family blessing begins with *meaningful touching.* It continues with a *spoken message* that attaches *high value* to the one being blessed. This message pictures *a special future* for the person and is based on an *active commitment* to see the blessing come to pass.

As we provide the five basic ingredients of the blessing, personal acceptance can thrive and bloom in a home or a life.

> *Jacob said to his father, "I am Esau your firstborn;*
> *I have done just as you told me; please arise, sit*
> *and eat of my game, that your soul may bless me."*
> —GEN. 27:19

What happens when people miss the blessing? This happens for a number of reasons. In fact, the blessing Isaac gave to Jacob was really a lost blessing because it was meant for Jacob's older brother, Esau. Because of Jacob's trickery (aided by his mother, Rebekah), Esau missed the blessing he had waited for all his life, the blessing that by custom belonged to him as the firstborn. Many years passed before he could come to terms with that loss.

In the next few days, we will explore some of the ways that missing the blessing can wreak havoc in our lives and relationships. But our purposes will be positive, not negative—to show the importance of the blessing. And remember, our Lord is a God of new beginnings. Even lost blessings can be redeemed.

What are some reasons that might cause a person to miss the blessing as a child or young adult?

When Esau heard the words of his father, he cried with an exceedingly great and bitter cry, and said to his father, "Bless me, even me also, O my father!"

—GEN. 27:34

Esau was horrified. *Could this really be happening?* Just hours before, his father, Isaac, had made a special request. If Esau, the older son, would catch fresh game and create a savory meal, Isaac would bestow his long-awaited blessing. With the skill of an experienced hunter, Esau had gone about his work. He had precisely followed directions. Why, then, had his father trembled so violently when Esau stood before him with the delicious stew?

"Who?" the old man had queried. "Where is the one who hunted game and brought it to me? I ate all of it before you came, and I have blessed *him*."

Gradually the ugly truth had dawned. Esau's younger brother, Jacob, had tricked Isaac into blessing him instead of Esau. And because a spoken blessing was then considered irretrievable, Esau could only beg, "Do you have only *one* blessing, my father? Bless me—me also!"

Can you feel Esau's anguish in his cry of unfulfilled longing? Let it motivate you to make sure those you love aren't cheated of their blessing.

> *Now it came to pass, when Isaac was old and his*
> *eyes were so dim that he could not see, that he*
> *called Esau his older son and said to him, "My*
> *son." And he answered him, "Here I am."*
>
> —GEN. 27:1

A few years ago, I (John) used to give my wife a break by taking our little daughter to the mall. We would wander around and look at the shops. And of course we'd occasionally stop for ice cream, fudge, soda, cookies, and other goodies. Then I would take Kari home, hyper from all that sugar, and deposit her with my wife.

Before long, the "one treat" rule went into effect.

Kari's favorite treat in the one-treat era used to be the gum ball machine. She loved to put in her money, turn the knob, and receive a giant, colorful ball that would puff out her cheek like a chipmunk. One day, though, we stopped at the gum ball machine, deposited the coin, turned the knob, and . . . no gum ball. We tried another coin, and another. Still no gum ball. And Kari looked at me in dismay. She had done her part. Why was the machine holding out on her?

That question was part of Esau's pain. He had been a good, obedient son, answering his father's call. Why couldn't he have his father's blessing?

"Why can't I have it?" is the inner cry—conscious or unconscious—of many people who are deprived of the blessing.

> *Look, he has taken away my blessing!"*
> —GEN. 27:36

Please say you love me, please!" Brian's words trailed off into tears as he leaned over his father's still form. Only the humming of a heart monitor responded.

All his life, Brian had searched in vain for his father's approval. A career Marine, Brian's father had worked hard to make his son as tough as he was—no words of tenderness or praise, just lectures on doing better. As a result, Brian grew up feeling inferior and rebellious. He was dishonorably discharged from the Marines. He worked at jobs far beneath his abilities and broke off three engagements just before the wedding. Finally he sought help and learned that he was experiencing common symptoms of growing up without a sense of family blessing.

When word came of his father's heart attack, Brian flew to his side immediately, hoping that, finally, they could reconcile their relationship. But Brian's father died without regaining consciousness. And Brian's sobs revealed his incredible sense of loss: not only of his father, but of his last chance at his father's blessing.

It's never too early to bless a child, but it can be too late.

> *So Esau hated Jacob because of the blessing with*
> *which his father blessed him.*
> —GEN. 27:41

Nancy's mother was elegant, petite, and socially in-
clined. Unfortunately, Nancy was a big-boned tomboy.
None of her mother's scoldings about being "clumsy"
or "fat" could turn her into a social butterfly like her
older sister. She grew up knowing she was a disappointment to her mother.

When Nancy came to us for counseling years later,
she struggled with deep-seated insecurities that made
her keep her loving husband at arm's length. But Nancy's deepest struggle involved her two daughters—an
older child who resembled Nancy and a dainty, petite
younger child.

Just as she had during Nancy's childhood, Nancy's
mother catered to the "pretty one." Nancy relived old
hurts as she saw the rejection her older daughter suffered. And though she fought it, Nancy found herself
resenting her youngest daughter. She also discovered
she was furious at God. She stopped going to church,
participating in Bible study, or even praying.

Bitterness, resentment, displaced relationships, and estrangement
from God can be results of a missed blessing.

*Then Isaac his father answered and said to him:
"Behold, your dwelling shall be of the fatness of the
earth, and of the dew of heaven from above. By
your sword you shall live, and you shall serve your
brother; and it shall come to pass, when you
become restless, that you shall break his yoke from
your neck."*

—GEN. 27:39–40

In response to his pitiful cries, Esau did receive a blessing of sorts from his father. But this was a kind of consolation prize—better than nothing, but not the words of value Esau had longed to hear.

Many people live with a consolation-prize blessing. They didn't miss out entirely, but neither did they grow up feeling fully blessed. Perhaps only one parent, or even another adult, gave them a blessing. Or possibly the child's expectations were too high for any human to fill.

But note the promise of freedom in Esau's blessing. It helps to remember *all* human blessings are consolation-prizes compared with the blessings of our perfect heavenly Parent. This doesn't make earthly blessings less important, but this realization can set us free us from the burden of blame or guilt. We are then free to seek a full blessing from God.

Those who hunger for God's blessings will not have to settle for a consolation prize.

> *Being confident of this very thing, that He who has*
> *begun a good work in you will complete it until the*
> *day of Jesus Christ.* —PHIL. 1:6

As you have started learning about benefits of the blessing and the pain of missing it, perhaps you have felt a little discouraged. Maybe you have realized for the first time that you never received the blessing from your parents. Or you have discovered it is not an active part of your relationship with your children. Maybe you've found another of your relationships is suffering because someone did not receive the blessing as a child.

If this is true, please don't lose heart. As you continue your daily exploration of the blessing, you will gradually gain practical skills to become a source of blessing to others. In the process, you will also discover how to deal effectively with the lack of blessing in your life. You will also encounter a wealth of specific ideas and models to help you bestow the blessing on children, your spouse, church family, and friends.

Remember you are very special to God as His precious child. He has promised to complete the good work He has begun in you. As you continue to grow in Him, He will teach you to be a blessing to others.

*You are sons . . . of the covenant which God made
with our fathers, saying to Abraham, "And in your
seed all the families of the earth shall be blessed."
To you first, God, having raised up His Servant
Jesus, sent Him to bless you, in turning away every
one of you from your iniquities.*

—ACTS 3:25–26

Is the blessing we build into a person's life today exactly like the blessing given in the Old Testament? No. While the basic relationship elements of blessing remain the same, the Scriptures contain several aspects of the blessing that were unique to that time. One way we can see the unique spiritual side of the family blessing is to look at how God used this concept to identify His life of blessing through one family until the coming of Christ.

God's covenant of blessing was originally made with and was to pass directly through one family's offspring. It began with Abraham, was passed on to his son, Isaac, to his son, Jacob, and so on. Generation after generation of Abraham's descendants received the blessing God had promised them. And this continued from one generation to the next right up to the Messiah's birth.

In contrast, because of what Jesus did for all people, now every family and each family member can experience a blessing through God's Son. This blessing can be passed on to others by introducing them to Christ.

Spiritually speaking, God's blessing is available to anyone who accepts Jesus Christ as Savior.

> *Now when Joseph saw that his father laid his right*
> *hand on the head of Ephraim, it displeased him; so*
> *he took hold of his father's hand to remove it from*
> *Ephraim's head to Manasseh's head . . . . But his*
> *father refused and said, ". . . Truly his younger*
> *brother shall be greater than he, and his*
> *descendants shall become a multitude of nations."*
> —GEN. 48:17,19

Another spiritual meaning associated with the blessing is how it pictures God's sovereign choice. With Jacob and Esau and with another set of brothers, Ephraim and Manasseh, God's sovereignty was pictured through who received the family's blessing and who did not. The Old Testament blessing also showed a prophetic element that does not apply to those of us giving the blessing today. For example, because of Jacob's unique position as a patriarch—God's appointed leader and a father of the nation of Israel—his words of blessing carried with them the weight of biblical prophecy. His blessing to his grandchildren and each of his sons revealed their future exactly as it would unfold.

Today, we cannot presume to indicate God's choice, nor can we predict another person's future with biblical accuracy.

God's choices remain in God's hands—and spiritual blessings come from Him.

Every man shall give as he is able, according to the blessing of the LORD your God which He has given you.

—DEUT. 16:17

Besides the unique spiritual meanings attached to the family blessing, the blessing always has an intensely personal side. This can be seen in Esau's heart-wrenching cries over losing his father's blessing. He was not crying over the loss of an objective theological concept, but over the deeply personal words from his father that had eluded him.

The personal, or relational, side of using the blessing to communicate parental love is the element orthodox Jewish homes have continued to practice by blessing children. Jewish parents recognized the unique spiritual and prophetic aspects of the blessing given by the patriarchs. But these orthodox homes adopted the basic relationship elements of the blessing to encourage their children. These tools communicate acceptance and still apply to men and women today.

In the personal or relational realm, our responsibility for passing on the blessing emerges.

> *And Jacob called his sons and said, "Gather*
> *together, that I may tell you what shall befall*
> *you. . . . And he blessed them; he blessed each one*
> *according to his own blessing.*
>
> —GEN. 49:1,28

In Old Testament times, each child in a family received a blessing from the parents. Although firstborn sons and daughters received additional privileges, all children received the essential elements of the blessings. That didn't mean the blessings were generic. Each blessing was tailored to fit the individual who received it.

In Genesis 49, for instance, each of Jacob's twelve sons received a blessing reflecting his particular personality and picturing his unique future. For instance: "Gad, a troop shall tramp upon him, but he shall triumph at last" (Gen. 49:19) or "Naphtali is a deer let loose; He gives goodly words" (Gen. 49:21).

Blessings are best when they are custom-made for the recipient.

> *If you then, being evil, know how to give good gifts to your children, how much more will your Father who is in heaven give good things to those who ask Him!*
>
> —MATT. 7:11

Around the time of Christ's birth, Rabbi Jesus ben Sirach wrote, "The blessing of the father builds houses for the sons; the blessing of the mother fills them with good things."

That tidbit of ancient wisdom carries much truth. One blessing is good. More than one blessing is even better. Each of us—father, mother, sibling, friend, pastor—has a unique touch and voice, a different perspective for attaching high value, a distinct vision of the future, a personal commitment. As a result, each of us can give a unique and priceless blessing. And we each are responsible to give it.

People benefit when any significant person in their lives makes the effort to give them a blessing. But people blossom when all the significant people in their lives give priority to blessing them.

> [*Jesus*] *said to them, "Let the little children come to*
> *Me, and do not forbid them . . . ." And He took*
> *them up in His arms, put His hands on them, and*
> *blessed them.*
> —MARK 10:14,16

During New Testament times, the Jewish people had rules and regulations for nearly every event—including the blessing of children. While a general blessing for children existed during this time, the people developed a trend of blessing sons instead of daughters. This tendency is seen in many of the Hebrew commentaries on the law of that era. One rabbi even wrote, "What is the interpretation of the words 'all things' in the Scripture, 'The Lord blessed Abraham in all things'? That he had no daughter!"

Still, some Jewish religious leaders, made exceptions in their homes. In fact, another man some called *rabbi* during this period welcomed both sons *and* daughters to receive His blessing. His blessing of children parallels the important elements of the family blessing. His name is Jesus.

Jesus knew that both little boys and little girls needed the elements of the blessing.

So [Jacob] blessed them that day, saying, "By you Israel will bless, saying, 'May God make you as Ephraim and as Manasseh!'" . . . . —GEN. 48:20

Among orthodox Jews today, at many Shabbat (Sabbath) services, the parents are asked to bring their children for a special blessing. The rabbi calls the children in the congregation forward. Acting on behalf of the parents, the rabbi lays his hand on the head of each child and recites words like these, "May God bless you and make you as Ephraim and Manasseh."

This blessing, the same blessing that Jacob gives to his two grandchildren in Genesis, is still a favorite for orthodox parents to use with their children. This blessing uses words directly from Scripture to praise a child and picture a wonderful future—a future in which the child plays a part in God's great plan.

Scripture is not only a source of blessing in itself. It is an abundant resource of words and images for us as we bless others.

Blessed is the man
Who walks not in the counsel of the ungodly.
—PS. 1:1

This is an example of a Scripture-based blessing you can use to express love, acceptance, and a positive picture to someone you love. This blessing uses the images of Psalm 1 to express high esteem and high hope:

How blessed you, _____(insert person's name)_____, will be because you do not walk in the counsel of the wicked, nor stand in the path of sinners, nor do you sit in the seat of scoffers. But as your parents, we have seen you delight in the law of the Lord. You have thought about His law day and night. May God make you, _____(person's name)_____, like a tree firmly planted by streams of water. May God allow you to grow and bear His fruit in His season and your life will not wither and whatever you shall do, it will prosper!

Today, read this blessing aloud with your name in the blanks. Then mark this page of the book and look for an opportunity to pass the same blessing to your spouse, one of your children, or a friend.

Surely My Sabbaths you shall keep, for it is a sign between Me and you throughout your generations.
—EX. 31:13

While studying how the blessing is given in modern Jewish homes, we spoke with several rabbis. In our interviews, we discovered the family blessing is considered an important vehicle for communicating a sense of identity, meaning, love, and acceptance. In fact, in many orthodox homes, a weekly blessing is given by the father to each of his children, usually as part of the Sabbath celebration. With the ceremonial candles lit, a time of blessing begins.

Sharing special meals; kissing, hugging, or the laying on of hands; creating a word picture or using one from the Scriptures to praise a child; even asking God to provide a special future for each child are common elements of blessing children in orthodox homes today.

———————————

From a blessing to the firstborn to special words of love and acceptance for each child, the blessing remains a vital part of Jewish family life. Christian parents who have the hope and reality of Jesus and His love can share a blessing that is even more powerful.

Give us this day our daily bread.
—MATT. 6:11

The family blessing described in the Old Testament—
the special blessing given by the patriarchs—was a formal occasion that took place at a special time in a
child's life. Similar "special" occasions can be intensely
meaningful in the lives of people we love. At the same
time, the blessing can and should be a part of everyday
life. People hungry for a blessing need daily bread as
well as special banquets!

In numerous seminars and counseling sessions, we
asked people: "What is one specific way you knew you
had received your parents' blessing?" Their responses
show the importance of a parent's everyday actions
and attitudes in communicating the blessing to their
children. Each small act of love and encouragement
was actually a decision a parent made to provide an
element of the blessing to a child. Even now, years
later, that blessing is still remembered and cherished.

Small acts of love and acceptance are the daily bread of blessing.

Who is wise and understanding among you? Let
him show by good conduct that his works are done
in the meekness of wisdom.
—JAMES 3:13

Earlier, we told you we asked people: "What is one way you knew you had your parents' blessing as you grew up?"

Their answers might help you as you bless your children:

1. My parents took the time to really listen to me when I talked to them. They would look directly into my eyes.
2. We were often spontaneously hugged.
3. They would let me explain my side of the story.
4. We went camping as a family. (This was a frequent response.)
5. They would take each of us for a special breakfast alone with them.
6. My father would put his arm around me at church and let me lay my head on his shoulder.
7. I got to spend one day at Dad's office, seeing where he worked and meeting his co-workers.
8. My mother carried pictures of each of us in her purse.
9. They would watch their tone of voice when they argued.

We never know what small acts of love and encouragement will mark someone's life.

> *Greet one another with a kiss of love.*
> —1 PETER 5:14

How would you like to lower your husband's or wife's blood pressure? Or protect your grade-school children from being involved in an immoral relationship later in life? Would you like to add up to two years to your own life? (Almost sounds like an insurance commercial, doesn't it?)

Actually, these are all findings in recent studies of the incredible power to bless. These are results of the first element of the blessing: *meaningful touch.* We give the people we care about an incredible gift when we dare to reach out and touch them.

This month, we will explore the promise and possibilities found in this first element of the blessing.

Touch us, O Lord, even as we reach out to touch each other in Your love.

Then his father Isaac said to him, "Please come close and kiss me, my son." —GEN. 27:26 NASB

In the Old Testament, touch played an important part in bestowing the family blessing. Isaac's blessing Jacob included an embrace and a kiss. Isaac instructed Jacob to "come close" for his blessing.

The Hebrew word for "come close" is very descriptive. It is used of armies drawn together in battle. It is even used to picture the overlapping scales on a crocodile's skin. Perhaps you haven't seen a battle or a crocodile for a while, but these examples still help us picture a very close connection.

Isaac wasn't asking Jacob for an "Aunt Ethel hug." (Remember Aunt Ethel—the one who pinched your cheek and repeatedly patted your back when she hugged you like you were a baby she was burping?) Free from the current taboos our culture sets on men embracing other men, Isaac was calling Jacob close to give him a bear hug!

Meaningful touch means daring to "come close" to those we love.

*Did You not . . . clothe me with skin and flesh, and
knit me together with bones and sinews? You have
granted me life and favor, and Your care has
preserved my spirit.* —JOB 10:10–12

A little girl became frightened one night during a
thunderstorm. After one particularly loud clap of thun-
der, she burst into her parents' room. Jumping into the
middle of the bed, she sought her parents' arms for
comfort and assurance.

"Don't worry, honey," her father said, trying to calm
her fears. "The Lord will protect you."

The little girl snuggled closer. "I know that, Daddy,
but right now I need someone with skin on!"

This little one did not doubt her heavenly Father's
ability to protect her, but she also knew He had given
her an earthly father. She knew she could run to this
one God had made and entrusted with a special gift to
bring her comfort, security, and personal acceptance—
the blessing of meaningful touch.

*We are privileged to give the gift of love and acceptance "with skin
on."*

In the beginning was the Word, and the Word was
with God, and the Word was God. . . . And the
Word became flesh and dwelt among us.
—JOHN 1:1,14

The Word made flesh. God become human. A deity with skin on—a God we can touch.

The theological term for that event is *incarnation*. This means the mighty God of the universe, the spirit beyond all comprehending, cared enough to live among us in human form. He came to hold children, lay healing hands on the sick, rub elbows with the poor, wash the feet of His disciples. His mission even included dying at human hands and redeeming that painful touch through His resurrection.

God's incredible gift of incarnation means so many things—redemption, salvation, hope. But surely it is also a powerful acknowledgment that our human need for meaningful touch was meant to be met.

Father, thank You that You came to us as a real human being. Even as You blessed the world with the touchable gift of Your incarnation, let us be instruments of Your healing, redeeming touch in a world that needs You more than ever.

> *Then He said to Thomas, "Reach your finger here,*
> *and look at My hands; and reach your hand here,*
> *and put it into My side. Do not be unbelieving, but*
> *believing." And Thomas answered and said to Him,*
> *"My Lord and my God!"*
>
> —JOHN 20:27–28

For children, things become real when they are touched. Have you ever been to Disneyland and watched a child's expression when he comes face to face with a person dressed like Goofy or Donald Duck? Even if the child is initially afraid, soon she will want to reach out and touch the Disney character. This same principle lets children stand in line for hours to see Santa Claus—the same children who normally can't sit still for five minutes. And this desire enables children to learn concepts that otherwise might never penetrate their minds—"hands on" learning is almost always more effective than simple "book learning."

Children aren't the only ones who need to touch to comprehend. Even Jesus' disciple, Thomas, had that acute need to touch before he could comprehend. And while Jesus gently chided him for his lack of faith, He also acknowledged the disciple's emotional need and said, "Reach your finger here . . ."

Meaningful touch has a way of making love concrete and believable.

*And [Jacob] came near and kissed [Isaac]; . . . and
[Isaac] blessed him.*
                                          —GEN. 27:27

Every child needs to be touched. And yet many par
ents (particularly fathers) stop touching their children
when the children reach the grade school years! When
this happens, an element of the blessing stops. Most
parents know a four-year-old needs to be cuddled. But
what about a fourteen-year-old's need to be meaningfully touched by his mother or father (even if the teenager outwardly cringes when he or she is hugged)? Or
how about the appropriate touching a thirty-four-year-
old needs? Or your spouse or a close friend?

How old was Jacob when our Scripture example
happened? Genesis 26:34 tells us that Esau married at
age forty, and this was before Isaac's blessing. Since
Jacob was Esau's twin, he must have been at least forty
years old when Isaac blessed him! And yet Isaac didn't
set age barriers around the need to be touched. His
blessing for his forty-year-old son came complete with
a hug or a kiss. He gives us a model that parents, husbands and wives, and even friends at church can follow in giving the blessing.

---

*We are never too old to benefit from receiving—and giving—mean-
ingful touch.*

> *Turn Yourself to me, and have mercy on me,*
> *For I am desolate and afflicted.*
> —PS. 25:16

I wish . . . I wish. . . ." Lisa slumped in her chair, hugging herself and rocking as she repeated these words. Lisa was a new adolescent patient in the psychiatric ward where I (John) was a seminary intern. Whenever she felt afraid or sad, she would wrap herself in her arms and rock.

Lisa had behaved this way since she was seven years old. At that time, her mother had abandoned her at an orphanage. Lisa tried to escape the pain she felt by holding herself. After all, she had no one else to hold her; all she had was the wish her mother would return. She needed meaningful touching so much that she would wrap her arms around herself and try to hug away the hurt.

Children are particularly affected by touch deprivation. Sometimes the absence of touch can so affect a child that he or she spends a lifetime reaching for embracing arms.

Pray for the children like Lisa who starve for touch. Then resolve to make meaningful touch an element of the blessing you extend to those you love.

*Then Israel stretched out his right hand and laid it
on Ephraim's head . . . and his left hand on
Manasseh's head.*
                                                    —GEN. 48:14

In the Scriptures, we find another clear example of
including meaningful touch while bestowing the blessing. This time the blessing involves a grandfather who
wanted to make sure his grandchildren received this
special gift of personal acceptance.

Jacob, whose name had now been changed to Israel,
not only kissed them and held them close, but He also
placed his hands on each grandson's head. This practice of laying on hands was important in many of the
religious rituals for the patriarchs and for Israel—and
it is still practiced in many churches.

Placing our hands on someone as part of the blessing is important for at least two reasons. First, a symbolic meaning is attached to touching, and second,
laying on hands actually carries tremendous physical
benefits.

*Have you ever been in a formal ceremony that involved the laying
on of hands? What part do you think the actual physical touch of
hands played in your reactions?*

> *Aaron shall lay both his hands on the head of the
> live goat, confess over it all the iniquities of the
> children of Israel . . . putting them on the head of
> the goat, and shall send it away into the
> wilderness. . . . The goat shall bear on itself all
> their iniquities.*
> —LEV. 16:21–22

In the Old Testament, the symbolic laying on of hands was important. This touch was a graphic picture of *transferring* power or blessing from one person to another.

In Leviticus, for example, Aaron was instructed to use this practice in his priestly duties. During the Day of Atonement, he was to place his hands on the head of a goat that was then sent into the wilderness. In so doing, he symbolically transferred the sins of Israel onto that animal. (This act is also a prophetic picture of how Christ, like that spotless animal, would shoulder our sins at the cross.) In a similar way, the laying on of hands can be a way of symbolically transferring a blessing from one person to another.

*When we lay our hands on someone in blessing, we symbolically
transfer our love and esteem—and God's blessing—to that person.*

> . . . *Jehu said, ". . . Give me your hand." So*
> *[Jehonadab] gave him his hand.*
>
> —2 KINGS 10:15

The way we touch each other carries tremendous symbolic meaning, even when we don't realize it. In the business world, for example, a handshake signals the completion of an important deal, or a mentor's friendly arm on a protégé's shoulder indicates protection and guidance.

Touch is even more vital in personal relationships. A woman who takes her boyfriend's hand, or a man who grasps a woman's elbow to steer her through a crowded restaurant, may signal, "I want to be close to you" as well as "You're mine." Even more significantly, joining a couple's hands during a wedding powerfully symbolizes the joining of their lives—that two people have truly become one flesh.

Think over the last few days. What interchanges did you witness in which touch carried symbolic meaning?

You therefore, my son, be strong.
—2 TIM. 2:1

As part of our speaking ministry, both of us spend much time in airports. As a result, airports have become favorite places to watch the symbolic meaning of touch.

Once we saw an entire family surrounding the oldest son. This young man was in the Army special forces and was heading overseas. Everyone hugged him repeatedly, except his father. The father would lay his hand on the son's shoulder or pat his back, but he just couldn't bring himself to hug his grown son in public. When it was time for this soldier to board the plane, his father held out his hand, and the two shook hands.

"Hug him!" we wanted to shout. After a moment, the father placed his other hand around his son's. For what seemed like forever, this father and son stood, hands clasped, letting this act of touch say their goodbyes. Talk about a symbolic message! Even if this father couldn't make himself hug his son, he had communicated a great deal.

Even a simple handshake from a loved one can shout the words, "I love you. Please, be careful. Be strong. And come back to us."

Let him kiss me with the kisses of his mouth—
for your love is better than wine.

—SONG 1:2

Valentine's Day is a celebration of love and devotion, hearts and flowers, and especially hugs and kisses. What better day to celebrate the blessing of meaningful touch?

Don't just stick with the obvious—a kiss with the cards and flowers. Offer a Valentine back rub or a foot massage. Scratch your six-year-old's back. Visit a nursing home to dispense some long-needed hugs, or volunteer to hold babies at a local hospital. Kidnap your spouse for a special romantic evening. Hold hands even if you haven't done so for years.

Whatever you do, resolve to use the blessing of meaningful touch to nurture your relationships and share God's love with others.

Lord, thank You for the blessing of meaningful touch. Teach me to "get physical" with those I love in ways that improve our lives and relationships.

> *They will lay hands on the sick, and they will*
> *recover.*
> —MARK 16:18

When Jacob blessed his grandchildren, they would long remember the symbolic act of his laying his hand on their heads. But symbolism is not the only important reason to touch. Touch also brings significant physical benefits.

In the Gospels, we repeatedly see Jesus reaching to touch people and to heal them physically. Even after He had ascended to heaven, His followers healed people in His name by touching them. The issue of "faith healing" today is controversial, even among Christians. But considerable scientific evidence supports the theory that physical touch does bring significant and positive physiological changes.

The power of touch in giving the blessing is literal as well as symbolic.

And when they had prayed, they laid hands on them.
—ACTS 6:6

Interestingly, the act of laying on hands has become the focus of much interest and research. Studies show, for instance, that touch can actually lower a person's blood pressure, cause the eyes to dilate, and raise the level of endorphins and beta blockers (the body's natural painkillers and tranquilizers).

Dr. Dolores Krieger, a professor of nursing at New York University who has studied the effects of laying on hands, has found the hemoglobin levels rise in both people's bloodstreams during this act.* Hemoglobin is the substance that carries oxygen to the tissues. An increase in hemoglobin levels, therefore, means more oxygen for body tissues. This energizes a person and can even aid the regenerative process if he or she is ill.

Even the simplest touch can bring physical blessings to both the one who touches and the one who is touched.

*Dolores Krieger, "Therapeutic Touch: The Imprimatur of Nursing," *American Journal of Nursing*, May 1975, p. 784.

> *And he arose and came to his father. But when he was still a great way off, his father saw him and had compassion, and ran and fell on his neck and kissed him.*
> —LUKE 15:20

Besides laying on hands, the Scriptures picture many other forms of meaningful touch. In both the Old and New Testaments, we see God's people touching each other—embracing, kissing, shaking hands. An earthy, healthy sense of physical connection exists that in no way lessens the spiritual connection.

In the parable of the Prodigal Son, Jesus even portrayed God's welcome of a returning sinner in terms of physical touch. Remember the story? The son left his family for a far country, wasted all his inheritance, and finally dragged himself home in shame. But the father was so overjoyed at his wayward son's return that he "fell on his neck and kissed him."

Most of us in our country—especially men—are too reticent when it comes to touch. However, the meaningful touch is so healthy! We should listen to Ralph Waldo Emerson: "I never like the giving of the hand, unless the entire body accompanies it!"

Today, give at least one hug you wouldn't normally give—to a child, to your spouse, to a friend.

Do not cast me off in the time of old age;
Do not forsake me when my strength fails.
—PS. 71:9

Some nursing homes can be dwellings of lonely despair. So can animal shelters. Residents of both can go for days or weeks without a meaningful touch. Thankfully, some nursing homes and animal shelters have made a dent in the loneliness by bringing seniors and pets together.

More often than not, these programs began as simple recreational activities. But it has quickly become apparent that nursing home residents who hold and touch pets live longer than those who don't. They also have a significantly more positive attitude about life. Those few hours a day when they have someone to touch, to talk to, to love, provide new life and energy for these aging folk.

We don't usually think of a mutt as being a source of blessing, but for some elderly people they are angels in disguise. Some nursing homes have even adopted their own "angels" to bring the blessings of touch to residents.

Animals can be healing sources of touch, but human touch is even more powerful. When you visit an elderly relative or a nursing home, make a special point to touch.

> *Orpah kissed her mother-in-law [Naomi], but Ruth*
> *clung to her.*
> —RUTH 1:14

A study at UCLA found that just to maintain emotional and physical health, men and women need eight to ten meaningful touches each day! This study also estimated that if some men would hug their wives several times a day, they could increase their life span by almost two years! (Not to mention what it would do for their marriages.)

But remember, we're talking about *meaningful* touches! At a marriage seminar I (Gary) conducted, I cited this UCLA study. A man in the second row reached over and began patting his wife on the shoulder, counting, "One, two, three . . ." That's not what I meant at all!

The UCLA researchers defined meaningful touching as a gentle touch, stroke, kiss, or hug given by significant people in our lives (a husband or wife, parent, close friend, and so on). They're referring to a touch that blesses and communicates—the difference between Orpah's dutiful kiss and Ruth's heartfelt embrace.

Lord, it's so easy for my touch to become dutiful and perfunctory—a peck on the cheek, a pro forma handshake, an "Aunt Ethel" hug. As I go through my daily activities, keep me aware of the life-giving property of meaningful touch.

You have put gladness in my heart.
—PS. 4:7

In an interesting study at Purdue University, librarians were asked to alternately touch and not touch the hands of students as they handed back library cards. Later, the students who were touched reported much more positive feelings about the library and librarian than those who were not touched.

A surgeon we know tried his own similar study as he made hospital rounds. He spent the same amount of time with each patient. With half the patients, however, he sat on their beds and touched an arm or leg as he asked how they were. With his remaining patients, he simply stood near the bed to talk. When questioned later, the people he had touched reported that he had spent nearly twice as much time with them as those he had not touched reported!

As these studies show, even small acts of touch can leave a lasting perception of love and acceptance. Touching a child on the shoulder when he or she walks in front of you; holding hands with your spouse when you wait in line; ruffling someone's hair—these small acts can change how others view you, themselves, and your relationship.

Even a tiny touch can put gladness into someone's heart.

For the Lord . . . will comfort all her waste places.
—ISA. 51:3

A free-lance reporter from the *New York Times* interviewed Marilyn Monroe years ago. The reporter was aware of Marilyn's past and knew she had been shuffled from one foster home to another during her early years. The reporter asked, "Did you ever feel loved by any of the foster families with whom you lived?"

"One," Marilyn replied, "when I was about seven or eight. The woman I lived with was putting on makeup, and I was watching her. She was in a happy mood, so she reached over and patted my cheeks with her rouge puff . . . For that moment, I felt loved by her."*

Marilyn Monroe had tears in her eyes when she remembered this event. Why? The touch lasted only a few seconds, and happened years earlier. The touch was casual, playful—not an attempt to communicate great warmth or meaning. But that small act felt like buckets of love and security poured over the parched life of a little girl who hungered for affection.

You never know what small touch can make a difference in someone's life.

*Helen Colton, *The Gift of Touch* (New York: Seaview/Putnam, 1983), p. 102.

*For I was hungry and you gave Me no food; I was
thirsty and you gave Me no drink.*

—MATT. 25:42

Parents, especially, must realize that neglecting to touch their children starves them of genuine acceptance. This neglect can even drive children into the arms of someone else who is all too willing to touch them. Analyzing why some young people are drawn to cults, one author writes:

> Cults and related movements offer a new family. They provide the follower with new people to worry about him, to offer him advice, to cry with him, and importantly, to hold him and touch him. Those can be unbeatable attractions.

Those certainly are powerful attractions, especially if meaningful touch has not been a part of the blessing a child receives at home.

Cults often entrap young people by offering them the meaningful touch they didn't experience in their own homes.

> *My bed will comfort me,*
> *my couch will ease my complaint.*
> —JOB 7:13

Even if children are not lured into a cult to make up for years of touch deprivation, they may be drawn into immoral relationships.

Many promiscuous men and women, people who work as prostitutes, and women who repeatedly have unwanted pregnancies have told researchers their sexual activity is merely a way to satisfy yearnings to be touched and held.

Psychiatrist Dr. Marc Hollender interviewed dozens of women who have had three or more unwanted pregnancies. Overwhelmingly, these women said they were "consciously aware that sexual activity was a price to pay to be cuddled and held." For them, touching before intercourse was more pleasurable than intercourse itself, "which was merely something to be tolerated."

We all need to be held. Children who don't have that need met in healthy ways may look for it in unhealthy ways.

And you did not allow me to kiss my sons and my daughters. Now you have done foolishly in so doing.
—GEN. 31:28

Meaningful touch may also play a part in determining sexual orientation. One study with homosexual men revealed a common characteristic: a lack of meaningful touch from their fathers early in life. Dr. Ross Campbell, in his excellent book, *How to Really Love Your Child,* finds a similar conclusion. He writes, "In all my reading and experience, I have never known of one sexually disoriented person who had a warm, loving, and affectionate father."

Admittedly, this issue raises many questions. Certainly, touch from both a mother and father is important. And not all people who grow up without a loving touch from one or both parents turn out to be homosexual.

Regardless, the key point holds. Meaningful touching can protect a child from looking to meet this need in all the wrong places.

Do you know someone whose hunger for touch has led them to the wrong places? Or is this a problem in your life? We have good news: God can redeem even a touch-deprived and gone-astray life!

> *Then they brought little children to Him, that He*
> *might touch them; but the disciples rebuked those*
> *who brought them. But when Jesus saw it, He was*
> *greatly displeased and said to them, "Let the little*
> *children come to Me, and do not forbid them; for of*
> *such is the kingdom of God . . ." And He took them*
> *up in His arms, laid His hands on them, and*
> *blessed them.*   —MARK 10:13–14, 16

If we ignore our children's, spouse's or close friends' physical and emotional needs for meaningful touch, we deny them an important part of the blessing. What's more, we shatter a biblical guideline that our Lord Jesus set in blessing others.

Meaningful touching was certainly part of Jesus' blessing the children. Mobbed by onlookers and protected by His disciples, Jesus could have easily just waved to the children or ignored them completely. But He didn't. Jesus would not even settle for the politician's "chuck under the chin" routine. Instead, He "took them up in His arms, laid His hands on them, and blessed them."

Jesus gives us a direct model to follow in blessing our children with meaningful touch.

> *Then Jesus called a little child to Him, set him in*
> *the midst of them, and said, "Assuredly, I say to*
> *you, unless you are converted and become as little*
> *children, you will by no means enter the kingdom*
> *of heaven."*
>
> —MATT. 18:2–3

Note the contrast between today's verse and yesterday's verse. When Jesus said, "Let the little children come to Me," He was *not* simply communicating a spiritual lesson to the crowds. If He was, He could have done so by simply placing one child in the center of the group as He did in today's verse.

No, in blessing the children, Jesus demonstrated His knowledge of a child's deep need to be held and touched and blessed. And He gave us a model we can all follow.

Dear Lord, thank You for Your example of blessing by meaningful touch. Please be with me today as I strive to pass on Your blessing by touching the people around me.

> *Now a leper came to Him, imploring Him . . . and*
> *saying to Him, "If You are willing, You can make*
> *me clean." Then Jesus, moved with compassion,*
> *stretched out His hand and touched him, and said*
> *to him, "I am willing; be cleansed."*
> —MARK 1:40–41

Jesus was a master at communicating love. He showed this by blessing and holding the little children. But another time, His sensitivity to touching people was even more graphic. This was when Jesus met a grown man's need for meaningful touch—a man who was barred by law from ever touching anyone again.

In Jesus' day, to touch a leper was unthinkable. People would not get within a stone's throw of lepers; in fact, they would *throw* stones to keep lepers away. Luke 5:12 tells us this man was covered with leprosy. His open sores were only partially hidden by dirty bandages. Yet before Christ even spoke to the man, His first kindness was to touch him.

Think about how this man must have longed for someone to touch him. Jesus could have healed him first and then touched him. But recognizing his deepest need, Jesus stretched out His hand.

Who are today's "untouchables"—the homeless, the defensive, the sick? Pray that God will help you see beyond the surface and see someone who is hungry for meaningful touch.

Be of one mind, having compassion for one
another . . . be tenderhearted, be courteous. . . .
that you may inherit a blessing.

—1 PETER 3:8–9

During the first day of an introductory speech class at a large university, the teacher asked students to introduce themselves by answering two questions: "What do I like about myself?" and "What don't I like about myself?"

Dorothy sat in the back, her long red hair hanging around her face. When her turn came, silence filled the air. The teacher moved nearer and gently repeated the question. No answer.

Finally, Dorothy pulled back her hair to reveal her face—half covered with a large, irregularly shaped birthmark. "That," she said, "should show you what I don't like about myself."

Compassionately, this godly professor hugged her, then kissed her cheek where the birthmark was. "That's okay, honey," he said, "God and I still think you're beautiful."

Dorothy cried uncontrollably for twenty minutes. She finally sniffed, "I've wanted so much for someone to hug me and say that. Why couldn't my parents? My mother won't even touch my face."

A simple act of meaningful touch can begin to heal years of heart-ache and loneliness.

> *To everything there is a season,*
> *a time for every purpose under heaven:* . . .
> *A time to embrace,*
> *and a time to refrain from embracing.*
> —ECCL. 3:1,5

Meaningful touch has an incredible power to heal, to protect, to communicate. But are there times when it's better to refrain from touching?

Unfortunately, as with any gift of God, the power of touch has been abused by some people. This powerful source of blessing has been turned into a curse in the form of physical or sexual abuse. And those who have been victims of this kind of touch may become acutely sensitive to and afraid of even casual touching—or they may misread the best of intentions.

This means all touch must be tendered with care and sensitivity. Not everyone is ready to receive a bear hug from a stranger or a casual acquaintance. It's not even a bad idea to ask, "Do you mind if I give you a hug?" Then, even if the answer is no, remain alert to ways of offering meaningful touch in less threatening ways.

Offer all the elements of the blessing with tenderness, compassion, and sensitivity. But remember, even those who have been hurt by painful touching still have the need for love "with skin on."

*We give thanks to God always for you all . . .
remembering without ceasing your work of faith,
labor of love, and patience of hope in our Lord
Jesus Christ in the sight of our God and Father.*
—1 THESS. 1:2–3

Here are some more examples, from those we surveyed, of daily blessings that can make all the difference in the life of someone you love:

1. My parents made sure each of us kids appeared in the family photos.
2. My parents would make a special Christmas ornament for each child that represented a character trait we had worked on that year.
3. When they were wrong, they admitted it and said "I'm sorry."
4. They had a "king or queen for a day" meal for us that would focus individual attention on each child.
5. My parents prayed for me even when I felt I didn't deserve it.
6. My folks wrote a special "story of my birth" and read it to me every year.
7. We read Psalm 139 as a family and discussed how God had uniquely and specially designed each of us children.

*We give thanks for you, too, as you persevere in faith, hope, and love
to extend an everyday blessing to those around you.*

> *That . . . I may speak boldly, as I ought to speak.*
> —EPH. 6:20

We have seen that meaningful touch provides a vital and healing element of the blessing. But touch is not enough. We also need to "speak boldly" the words of blessing that people are hungry to hear.

Touch is powerful, but touch can also be ambiguous. A kiss, a hug, a touch on the hand may not always be healing—remember, Judas betrayed Jesus with a kiss. And some people interpret even an innocent touch as a threat. For these reasons, meaningful touch must be undergirded with speech if it is to be truly effective in extending a blessing.

Can you think of an instance in your life when a well-meaning touch was misinterpreted? How could well-chosen words have avoided the problem?

GOD OF THE SPOKEN WORD – *March 4*

"For I have spoken," says the Lord GOD.
—EZEK. 26:5

Throughout the Old Testament, we find a keen recognition of the power and importance of spoken words. In the very beginning, God "spoke" the world into being. His covenant with the Hebrew people began with a promise and a blessing spoken to Abraham. He spoke to Moses through the burning bush, then continued to speak words of instruction and guidance to His people in the wilderness. Even after the Israelites arrived in the Promised Land, He continued to speak to them through their long and troubled history. Through His prophets, He sent words of warning and of consolation.

Finally, He sent us His Son—the Word made flesh— to communicate His love and complete His plan of salvation. And He continues to guide us through His written word, the Bible.

God has always been a God who communicates His blessings through spoken words. We who are created in His image, and redeemed through His Son, should do no less.

Do you think of yourself as a "person of the spoken word"? Do meaningful words come easily to you, or do you have to struggle to express them?

> *Do not withhold good from those to whom it is*
> *due, when it is in the power of your hand to do so.*
> —PROV. 3:27

Many parents hold a tragic misconception. They think their simply being present communicates the blessing. Nothing could be farther from the truth. A blessing becomes so only when it is put into words.

Abraham spoke his blessing to his son Isaac. Isaac spoke a blessing to his son Jacob. Jacob gave a verbal blessing to each of his twelve sons and to two of his grandchildren. The tradition of a spoken blessing has continued through the centuries. It is built in to the way we human beings operate.

To see the blessing bloom and grow in the life of a child, spouse, or friend, we must do more than just mean well. We must verbalize our message.

Good intentions are not enough. To provide genuine acceptance, we need to turn good intentions into spoken blessings.

The light of the eyes rejoices the heart, and a good report makes the bones healthy. —PROV. 15:30

Do you know why a light bulb comes on when you flip the switch? You have completed an electronic circuit by closing the loop so the electricity can flow freely. Energy is exchanged, and the light glows brightly.

Verbalizing a blessing produces the same effect on an emotional level. Somehow it "closes the circuit" of love and commitment and lets the energy of acceptance flow freely. Until we verbalize our love to our children, spouse, or friends, they may be aware the love is present, but they may not be able to feel it at work. However, when we "flip the switch" by using words, we close the loop of love—and their faces light up!

―――――――――――

What specific kinds of verbal blessings tend to light the eyes of those closest to you? Why do you think those particular messages are so effective?

And thus the secrets of his heart are revealed.
—1 COR. 14:25

I (John) grew up without a father at home. For a time, my grandfather was a father figure for me and my brothers. Grandfather was stern with white hair and a big beard (he looked a little like Robert E. Lee), and he was a firm disciplinarian. I was always a little afraid of him.

One day I had broken a rule and received the standard punishment—two swats with Grandfather's belt. I was still nursing my pride when I was sent to call Grandfather to dinner. I started to knock on his door, then saw it was open a crack. I pushed the door open. Grandfather was sitting on the edge of the bed, crying. I just knew I was in more trouble for catching him crying. But he beckoned me to him and took me in arms. "John," he said, "I just want you to know, it hurts me so much to have to discipline you boys. But I love you so much, and I want you to grow up to be good young men."

Grandfather died eight months later. But before he left us, I got to hear the love and commitment in my grandfather's heart. That day is still a red-letter day in my memory.

Providing for children and disciplining them are important expressions of love. But it's a lucky child who can also say, "I got to hear the words!"

Let each one of you speak truth with his neighbor,
for we are members of one another. —EPH. 4:25

My kids are great! But if I told them I think so, they might get a big head."

"Of course I love my wife. I married her, didn't I? I'm just not the type to make a big deal of things."

"Oh, he knows how I feel. I don't have to tell him."

Those are common statements. Some harbor a grain of truth. And yet the attitude that lies behind them— that communicating love is optional—can be deadly. It's not enough to love another person, be proud of that person, and want God's best for him or her. If we want to give the blessing to those we care about, to feed their hunger for acceptance and affirmation, we must "speak truth" to them by *communicating* our love, esteem, and commitment in a way they can hear.

"Speaking truth" is not just a matter of not lying. "Speaking truth" also involves "speaking up" and telling people how much they mean to us and to God.

Open rebuke is better than love carefully concealed.
—PROV. 27:5

The spoken blessing is particularly important in giving or gaining family approval. Many people clearly remember words of praise their parents spoke years ago. Others remember negative words they heard— and the memories are so vivid that they even remember what their parents were wearing when they spoke them!

Children who must fill in the blanks when it comes to what their parents think about them will often fail the test when it comes to feeling valuable and secure. This is also often true of friends and marriage partners. Spoken words give the hearer a clear indication that he or she is worthy of attention.

"But I don't yell at my children or criticize them like some parents do," you may say. Unfortunately, as today's Scripture implies, even a lack of negative words does not translate into a spoken blessing. A steady diet of "open rebuke" is certainly not healthy for a relationship, but honest communication is preferable to no communication at all. When it comes to giving the blessing, silence is not golden.

What specific words of praise or blame do you remember from your years of growing up? Why do you think those words had such an impact on you?

Then he sent messengers to Balaam . . . saying . . .
"For I know that he whom you bless is blessed, and
he whom you curse is cursed."   —NUM. 22:5–6

I (John) first learned the lesson of the spoken word on the football field. When I began playing football in high school, one coach constantly chewed me out. He even took extra time after practice to point out my mistakes. Once, after I missed an important block in practice, this coach stood right in my face and screamed at me incessantly. Then he sent me to the sidelines, where I stood next to a third-string player who rarely got into the game. I complained, "I wish he would get off my case."

"Don't say that," my teammate replied. "At least he's talking to you. If he ever stops, that means he's given up on you."

Many adults we see in counseling interpret their parents' silence in exactly the same way. Their parents may have loved them and provided for them. But without spoken words of blessing, they are left unsure of their personal worth and acceptance.

Like Balaam, we have the power to extend blessings through the power of the spoken word. Or, by withholding words of blessing, we leave others feeling like "third-string" people.

Out of the same mouth proceed blessing and cursing.
—JAMES 3:10

Do you remember the old saying, "Sticks and stones may break my bones, but words will never hurt me"? It's a lie!

As most of us learn too quickly, words *can* hurt. They can wound us deeply, destroy friendships, even rip apart a home or marriage. On the other hand, words have a unique power to build us emotionally, as well as to comfort and encourage. Words have the power to bless.

If you are a parent, your children desperately need to hear a spoken blessing from you. If you are married, your wife or husband needs to hear words of love and acceptance on a regular basis. This very week as you spend time with a friend, a co-worker, or someone at your church, you will rub shoulders with someone who needs to hear a word of encouragement. Speak up!

Think about a specific person in your life who could use a spoken word of blessing from you. Write down what you can say to that person and mark on your calendar (within the next week) a day and time to say it.

> *Indeed, we put bits in horses' mouths that they may obey us, and we turn their whole body. . . . Even so the tongue is a little member and boasts great things.*
>
> —JAMES 3:3,5

Today's verse contains one of James's three vivid word pictures that grab our attention and point out the power of spoken words.

Here, our tongue is pictured as a "bit" used to direct a horse. If you control a horse's mouth with a small bit, the entire animal will move in the direction you choose. (We have ridden a few horses who seem to be exceptions, but the general rule is certainly true.)

Just as the bit controls the horse and steers it in the right direction, the tongue has amazing power to direct and control a person or relationship. Through our spoken words of blessing, we can steer a child away from trouble, provide guidance to a friend, minister words of encouragement, or lift words of praise.

What kinds of words are most effective in steering your children, your mate, or your friends? Pray that your words will be influential and positive, never manipulative.

> *Look also at ships: although they are so large and*
> *are driven by fierce winds, they are turned by a*
> *very small rudder wherever the pilot desires. Even*
> *so the tongue is a little member and boasts great*
> *things.*
> —JAMES 3:4–5

Yesterday we looked at a word picture that illustrates the power of the tongue to control and direct persons and relationships. This second word picture in James, that of a ship's rudder, illustrates the same principle in a different way—and adds another dimension to the "steering" power of the tongue. When the rudder of a ship is used with care and skill, good results occur. But careless or inept steering brings tragic consequences: a collision, a wreck against the rocks, or—more recently—an oil spill that blackens the environment, kills wildlife, and lingers on the landscape for years to come.

Similarly, although our words have tremendous power for good, they can also be misused, sometimes with tragic results.

What are some of the "hot button" words that steer your relationships to the rocks? Make a list of them and pray for the discipline and self-control to avoid those words whenever possible.

See how great a forest a little fire kindles! And the tongue is a fire, a world of iniquity. . . . and sets on fire the course of nature.
— JAMES 3:5–6

This verse uses yet another word picture. It illustrates the way spoken words can burn deeply into a person's life, often setting the course that person's future will take.

That was certainly the case with Mean Mike. His family began calling him "Mean Mike" when he was just a toddler because, whenever anyone tried to take something away from him, he would snarl and hold on for dear life. The nickname began as a humorous way to picture his bulldog tenacity. But as Mike grew older, everyone still called him "mean." And gradually, constantly hearing he was mean burned itself into his character. At home and at school, he was a bully—too tough to get close to anyone, furious if anyone crossed him. The meanness gave him an edge on the football field, but wreaked havoc in his personal life. Today "Mean Mike" is in a state prison.

Children tend to live up to what we say about them. That's reason enough to choose our words carefully.

> *Let the words of my mouth and the meditation of*
> *my heart be acceptable in Your sight, O LORD, my*
> *strength and my Redeemer.*
> —PS. 19:14

Perhaps in your life, you still stumble over hurtful words your parents, spouse, or a close friend spoke to you—or negative words you have spoken to yourself. If so, these words fill your memory over and over, pointing you in a direction in life you don't want to follow. Perhaps you fear these word-memories hinder your ability to speak words of blessing to those you love.

If so, don't lose hope. As you learn more about the blessing, you can begin to hear and speak words that can lead to a new course in life. Horseback riding, navigation, and fire fighting—to use the images we have explored the past few days—are all learnable skills.

Make a list of words that haunt you from your past. As you proceed through the next devotionals, pray daily that those negative words can be erased and replaced by positive words, steering you in a good direction.

Do not say, . . . "Tomorrow I will give it," when you
have it with you.
—PROV. 3:28

In many homes today, a thief steals from our children. This marauder takes the precious gift of genuine acceptance and leaves confusion and emptiness. This villain masquerades as "fulfillment," "accomplishment," and "success," but its real name is *overactivity.* It can keep parents so busy that the blessing is never spoken, even with parents who dearly love their children. As one woman pointed out, "Who has time to stop and *tell* them?"

In many homes today, both parents are working overtime, and "family night" makes an appearance about as often as Halley's comet. As a result, instead of Dad and Mom taking the time to communicate a spoken blessing, a baby-sitter named *silence* molds a child's self-perception. Life is so hectic for many parents that the "just right" time to communicate a spoken blessing never arrives.

Spoken words of blessing should start in the delivery room and continue through life. Yet the lack of time and the thief's motto, "I'll have time to tell them tomorrow," rob children of a needed blessing today.

*Therefore comfort each other and edify one
another, just as you also are doing.*
—1 THESS. 5:11

A father tries to corner his son to communicate "how
he feels about him" before he goes away to college,
but now his son is too busy to listen.

A mother tries to express a spoken blessing to her
daughter in the bride's room just before the wedding,
but the photographer has to take her away to get that
"perfect" shot.

Or someone stands beside a new grave, with unsaid
words of love and acceptance bitterly melting on the
tongue.

On the other hand, consider the young woman, wid-
owed at age thirty after just a year of marriage. Although the pain of her loss is intense, she still has a
remarkable advantage. "I miss him so much," she says,
"but at least I don't have any regrets. We told each
other every day how much we meant to each other."

---

*Make it your goal to come to the end of your parenting years, and
to the end of your life, with no regrets over words of blessing you
haven't spoken.*

> *There is one who withholds more than is right,*
> *But it leads to poverty.*
> —PROV. 11:24

Oh, it's not that big of a deal," you may say. "My kids (or spouse, or friends) know I love them. They realize they're special without my having to say it."

Really? We wish that explanation worked with many of the people we counsel. To them, their parents' silence has communicated something far different from love and acceptance. And in many cases, the absence of spoken words has led to a kind of poverty that has little to do with money.

Over the next few days, we will examine what commonly happens in homes that withhold spoken words of blessing. We will see that silence does communicate a message; and like an eloquent speech, silence can set a course for a person's life. Unfortunately, this is not the path most parents would like their children to take.

What are some of the consequences of a withheld spoken blessing that you can imagine (or have seen)?

> *Now I rejoice, not that you were made sorry, but that your sorrow led to repentance. For you were made sorry in a godly manner, that you might suffer loss from us in nothing.* —2 COR. 7:9

Many branches of the Christian church are now celebrating the season of Lent, a time of preparation leading to the joy of Easter. Traditionally, this is a time for reflection, self-examination, and repentance. It's a time to say both "I'm sorry" and "I want to change."

Those are appropriate sentiments for anyone who truly wants to bless others. Because we are human, we hurt each other—and often the ones we hurt most deeply are those we love the most. We lash out in anger. We fail to keep a promise. We take each other for granted. Brick by brick, our thoughtless or cruel actions build a wall of estrangement blocking the blessings we want to give. We only start taking down that wall when we learn to repent. And it's not enough to say it in our hearts. If we really want to bless our children, our spouse, our friends, we must learn to speak the words.

In this season of repentance, pray for the grace to say "I'm sorry."

Let the husband render to his wife the affection due her, and likewise also the wife to her husband.
—1 COR. 7:3

Today's verse refers specifically to sexual needs in a marriage, but it can apply just as surely to the need for spoken words of love and affection.

Dr. Howard Hendricks, a noted Christian educator, is fond of telling the story of a couple he counseled several years ago. This couple had been married for more than twenty years, but their problems had become so acute that they were considering divorce.

Dr. Hendricks asked the husband, "When was the last time you told your wife you love her?" The man glared at him, crossed his arms, and announced, "I told my wife I loved her on our wedding day, and it stands until I revoke it!"

Guess what was destroying that couple's marriage! When a spoken blessing is withheld in a marriage, unmet needs for security and acceptance can act like sulfuric acid and eat away at a relationship.

When was the last time you told your spouse—or another special person in your life—how much you love him or her? Make a point of saying it at least once a day for the next week.

You have sown much, and bring in little . . . and he who earns wages, earns wages to put into a bag with holes.
—HAG. 1:6

Individuals, as well as relationships, suffer from the lack of a spoken blessing. Without words of love, acceptance, and encouragement, children often grow up traveling one of two roads that lead to unhealthy extremes. Dan, for example, took the road marked, "Try a little harder."

Dan grew up in a home where few positive words were ever said—in fact, little of *anything* was said. His parents seemed too busy with their careers to talk much. But one exception to this general rule came when Dan received an excellent report card in grade school. For the first time in his memory, his parents openly praised him. Dan finally felt like somebody. Not surprisingly, Dan spend the rest of his school years overachieving. Then he carried his need for acceptance into the work force and became a "perfect" junior executive. While Dan would never admit it (inside he always knew it), pulling into his parents' driveway in a new car or talking about his new office was just another ploy to try to win their blessing.

Workaholism is often a repeated—but fruitless—attempt to secure a blessing withheld in childhood.

For they were employed in that work day and night.
—1 CHRON. 9:33

A driven person may build an impressive list of accomplishments. But like Moses' fading glory, these achievements cannot sustain a missing sense of personal acceptance. So the person in question forever must make one more deal, sell one more product, take one more class, or attend one more motivational seminar. Unfortunately, "one more" is never enough to make up for a missed blessing early in life.

A key to bringing order into such a person's private world is coming to grips with missing out on the blessing. Until that happens, the driven man or woman's search for personal acceptance will keep him or her on the barren road to success and away from the pathway of life.

Does this description of a driven person ring true for you or for anyone else you know?

> *Death and life are in the power of the tongue.*
> —PROV. 18:21

A little boy lies dead in the snow. That was the disturbing opening scene of a film I (John) saw years ago. This was the true story of Roger, whose world fell apart and cost him his life.

Roger did well his first few years of school, until problems began at home. Then his parents divorced, his mother remarried, and his new stepfather, jealous for his wife's attention, limited the time she spent with Roger. Predictably, Roger's schoolwork suffered and his teachers, tired of his apparent apathy, gave up on him and left him to work alone. He withdrew from other children, and soon they ignored him. Gradually Roger retreated into a world of silence until finally, unable to stand the pain any longer, Roger collapsed on his way to school and died.

Roger's story is an extreme example of a second road often traveled by people who fail to hear a blessing—the road of apathy, depression, and withdrawal. For Roger was not killed by an infirmity, nor by a physical wound. He was killed by a lack of affirmation. He died for lack of a blessing.

Are words, or the lack of them, really that powerful? Solomon thought so. Like throwing ice water in our faces, he shocks us into reality by reminding us that our words can even hold the power of life and death.

I was mute with silence,
I held my peace even from good.
—PS. 39:2

If spoken words of love and acceptance are so important, why are they offered so infrequently? Here are
a few reasons we have gathered from people we have
counseled:

"I don't want to inflate my child's ego."

"I'm afraid if I praise them, they'll take advantage
of me."

"Communication is too much like work. I work all
day, then she expects me to work all night talking to
her."

"I just don't know what to say."

"If I start, I'll have to make a habit of it."

If truth were known, however, the reason many people hesitate to verbally bless their children and others
is very simple: their parents never gave them this part
of the blessing. As in the days of the patriarchs, the
blessing, or lack of it, seems to trickle down through
generations.

If you never heard words of support and caring, you will struggle
with speaking them yourself. Nevertheless, if you have lips that move
and a mouth that speaks, or even a hand to write with, you can learn
to verbalize the blessing.

The statutes of the LORD are right, rejoicing the heart; The commandment of the LORD is pure, enlightening the eyes.

—PS. 19:8

Every family operates by certain "rules." These rules make up "the way our family does things," and cover all kinds of topics—what we eat, what TV programs we watch, how we observe holidays (for example, do we open presents on Christmas Eve or Christmas morning?), and how we communicate. Many marital arguments have gone fifteen rounds to see whose family rule will win out in the new marriage.

In some cases, family rules can be very helpful. For example, families can adopt biblical rules. These are "statutes of the Lord," like not letting the sun go down on anger and being kind to one another. These types of family guidelines can be safely passed through generations. But not all family rules are worth retaining. Some family rules—written or unwritten—can devastate a family. And one of the most common of these deadly rules is "Don't speak a blessing."

Make a list of some of the rules you followed in your family. Have any of these been objects of contention with someone you love?

A wholesome tongue is a tree of life.
—PROV. 15:4

All right, I'm convinced," you may say at this point, "but it's not that easy."

And you may be right for several reasons. Perhaps you've gone so long without a spoken blessing that words feel awkward and strange. Perhaps your kids are at a difficult stage and resist you. Or perhaps you simply feel inadequate to express how much you care—you find yourself at a loss for words when you try to speak a blessing.

Take hope: it gets easier with practice! In the meantime, you can transmit your words of blessing to the ones you love through other means.

1. Write a letter or a poem. Either read it aloud or simply hand it over. If at all possible, stay in the room while it is being read—and don't forget the blessing element of meaningful touch!

2. Speak your blessing on an audio or video tape. Or write a song and sing it! Get the words across the best way you can. You can trust God with the result.

Do whatever is necessary to be a tree of life for those you love by verbalizing a blessing to them.

> *Always pursue what is good both for yourselves*
> *and for all.*
> —1 THESS. 5:15

When Cherryl was growing up, a simple plaque hung in the family room. Its two hand-painted words—*Stand Up*—represented a three-generation family rule: "Stand up and fight. Don't take anything off anyone." Cherryl's father, for instance, had been infected with the "never give an inch" attitude of *his* father. He and Cherryl's mother fought constantly, and as the kids grew older they joined the battle, too.

Then Cherryl became a Christian and began chipping away at the family rule. Right in the middle of a fight, for instance, she would say, "I'm sorry. You're right. Will you forgive me?" She made a point of hugging her parents and telling them how much she loved them. Bit by bit, things began to change.

Cherryl's father had never received the blessing from his parents, only a plaque that almost destroyed him and his family. But over the next two years, he received the blessing from Cherryl. Finally, last Christmas, as a baby Christian, he took down the "Stand Up" plaque. Now Cherryl's family is free to "speak up" and share words of blessing with each other—because of one child's courage to battle a hurtful rule of silence.

What a testimony to God's power to break even the most difficult family rule!

*So teach us to number our days, that we may gain
a heart of wisdom*
—PS. 90:12

Have you ever attended a family reunion? For the first two days of these gatherings, everyone is generally talking up a storm about this recipe, that football team, this book they've read, or that movie to attend. But something happens the last afternoon of the reunion. Suddenly, with only an hour left before family members say their good-byes, meaningful words begin to fill the air. A brother will say in private to his sister, "I know things will work out in your marriage. I'll be praying for you." An aunt will say to her niece,"I know school is hard, but you can do it. I believe in you." Or a daughter will say to a parent, "Look around you, Mom. We didn't turn out half bad, did we? We have you and Dad to thank."

Many times we have to face a time pressure before we say the things closest to our hearts. But in your relationships with your children, your spouse, your close friends, even with your parents, it may be later than you think.

If you knew you only had an hour left with a loved one, what would you say to him or her?

> *But exhort one another daily, while it is called "Today."*
> —HEB. 3:13

While we wrote *The Blessing*, a tragic airplane crash in Japan killed more than five hundred people. One of them, a middle-aged Japanese man named Hirotsugu Kawaguchi, took his last few moments of life to write a note to his family. This note was found on his body at the wreckage site and finally made its way to his family:

> I'm very sad, but I'm sure I won't make it. The plane is rolling around and descending rapidly. There was something like an explosion that has triggered smoke. . . . Ysuyoshi [his oldest son], I'm counting on you. You and the other children be good to each other, and work hard. Remember to help your mother. . . . Keiko [his wife], please take good care of yourself and the children. To think our dinner last night was our last. I am grateful for the truly happy life I have enjoyed.*

Hirotsugu Kawaguchi left his family with words of blessing that will provide a positive echo in their lives for years to come. But such words of blessing need not be last words!

Time passes so quickly. Please don't let that important person leave your life without hearing the second element of the blessing—spoken words.

*Jack Burton, "Goodbye . . . Be Good to each other." Article in *USA Today*, August 19, 1985, p. 1.

Your words have upheld him who was stumbling,
And you have strengthened the feeble knees.
—JOB 4:4

Spoken words of blessing are so vital. They fortify re-lationships. They nurture and bolster self-esteem. They stimulate growth. And sometimes they can keep a worn-out traveler from stumbling on the road of life.

These worn-out travelers surround us. For instance, consider the wife and mother who is exhausted from juggling the demands of family, house, and job. Think of the discouraged teen who is slipping behind in school. How about the minister who faces burnout from being on call twenty-four hours a day. Remember the teacher drowning in a sea of paperwork. And of course, the depressed senior, the panicky mid-lifer, the lonely child. You, too, perhaps.

For all of these weary pilgrims, a few carefully cho-sen words of comfort, encouragement, empathy, or in-sight—perhaps accompanied by a hug—can make all the difference between stumbling and moving on.

Can you think of anyone in your circle of acquaintances who may be about to stumble? Pray that God will open your eyes to those in need of a word of blessing from you.

Is there no limit to windy words?
—JOB 16:3 NASB

We put spoken words of blessing into practice in our homes and relationships by deciding to speak up rather than clam up. Good intentions aside, encouraging words are necessary to bestow the blessing on a child, spouse, or friend.

But please note: We are not simply saying that you should talk more to your children or others. That is normally a good idea. But if you don't know how to communicate positively, you can say less by saying more. Your words become "windy words," appropriate to the month of March.

Not just *any* words, but words of high value attach themselves to a person and communicate the blessing. Sometimes these are the hardest words to say in the rush of everyday life. But they are the kind of words that must not be omitted if we want to give the blessing.

It's not how much you talk that gives the blessing, but what you say.

She, supposing Him to be the gardener, said to Him, "Sir, if You have carried Him away, tell me where You have laid Him, and I will take Him away." Jesus said to her, "Mary!" She turned and said to Him, "Rabboni!" (which is to say, Teacher).
—JOHN 20:15–16

Jesus was the center of her world. He had turned her life around. She had followed Him for many months. From Him, she had learned the real meaning of love.

And yet she didn't even know who the man was until she heard His voice.

From a very early age, even in the womb, we are attuned to voices. Before our mothers (and fathers) hold us for the first time, we know the sound of their voices. Researchers tell us newborns will unerringly turn toward their mother's voice. They also tell us that every human voice has an unique, unmistakable print.

Voices aren't interchangeable. Any old voice won't do. Perhaps that's why one of the sweetest sounds on earth is that of someone we love speaking words of blessing.

The sound of a well-loved voice gives words of blessing their special richness and power.

> *To everything there is a season. . . .*
> *A time to keep silence,*
> *and a time to speak.*
> —ECCL. 3:1,7

Let's look at some more answers people gave when we asked about how their parents blessed them. Which of the following daily blessings require spoken or written words? Could the "nonverbal blessings" be even more powerful accompanied by a spoken message?

1. They attended all of my open houses at school.
2. My father loved me by loving my mother.
3. My parents would tell us character traits we possessed that would help us be good marriage partners when we grew up and got married.
4. Mother would tell us "make believe" bedtime stories that illustrated positive character traits she felt we had.
5. They tried to be consistent in disciplining me.
6. Mom was always willing to help me with my math homework.
7. My folks tried to help me think through where I should go to college.
8. My parents' open discussion helped me set limits in the sex area.

This is the season to speak a blessing!

Esteem them very highly in love.
—1 THESS. 5:13

Nineteen-year-old Diane was born with a handicap. Her left arm never developed beyond the elbow. In her nineteen years, she has faced her share of obstacles from physical barriers, to stares, to fears about dating.

But Diane also lives with a tremendous advantage. From the day she was born, she has received a precious and powerful gift from her parents. They have given her the security of knowing she is highly valued and unconditionally accepted.

"My parents didn't try to shelter me from the fact that I was different," Diane told us. "They have been very realistic. But I always knew, and they have told me over and over again, that I am their greatest claim to fame. Whether I was trying out for softball or learning to drive, they have been my biggest fans. They have prayed for me and thought the best, even when I've pouted and gotten angry at God because of my handicap. Without question, my parents deserve credit for helping me accomplish the things I have."

The third element of the blessing is the one Diane's parents gave her. They blessed her by making sure she knew how much they valued her.

> *And he made his camels kneel down outside the*
> *city by a well of water at evening time.*
> —GEN. 24:11

To value something means to attach great importance to it. This is the very heart of the concept of blessing someone. When we extend the blessing to someone for whom we care, we say, both to ourselves and to the other person, that we believe he or she is very important.

In an earlier devotional, we saw that the Hebrew word translated "bless" means "to honor." The actual root meaning is to "bow the knee" the same root word used of the man with his camels in today's verse. In relationship to God, the word came to mean "to adore with bended knees"* as in "Bless the Lord, O my soul." When we "bless the Lord," we recognize God's intrinsic worth, acknowledging that He is worthy of our "bowing the knee" to Him. But the word also applies to blessing other people. Bowing before someone is a graphic picture of highly valuing that person.

Notice the important principle here: Anytime we bless someone, we attach high value to him or her.

*Brown, Drive, and Briggs, *Hebrew Lexicon,* p. 139.

Worthy is the Lamb who was slain
to receive power and riches and wisdom,
and strength and honor and glory and blessing!
—REV. 5:12

Spring is Easter season. And thoughts of Easter put the whole concept of honoring others into a slightly different perspective. Easter is the triumphant reality that gives the blessing an eternal edge and gives hope to those who miss the blessing on earth.

Blessing others by attaching high value to them pays tremendous emotional and relational dividends. But the highest value of all must belong to "the Lamb who was slain." He must receive our highest blessings. And only in Him can we find the love we need to bless others faithfully and unselfishly.

Today, take a break from working to bless others. Concentrate your thoughts of blessing on the Lord, praising Him, thanking Him, bowing your knee to Him.

> *Let each esteem others better than himself.*
> —PHIL. 2:3

Attaching high value to someone goes deeper than our feelings about that person. Extending a blessing means making a statement about the person's intrinsic worth and a decision about our attitude toward him or her.

Here's an example. In my life, I (Gary) want God to be of utmost value to me. On a 1 to 10 scale, I would value the Lord at 10. Next in line would come my relationship with Norma, my wife. Humanly speaking, she is my best friend, and I love and value her right beneath my love for the Lord—maybe a 9.5. Next come my children. I love each of them dearly and would value them at about a 9.4, right behind Norma.

Now, at times, say, after a week of camping in the rain, my feelings for my kids, my wife, or even God might drop to a 6.4 or even a 4.2. But during those moments, because I don't want to offend, hurt, or devalue these ones I love, I make the conscious decision to push their value back to where it belongs. I decide to honor them by extending a blessing to them.

The sentiment bears repeating: When we bless someone, we decide he or she is highly valuable, regardless of how we might feel on a moment-to-moment basis.

Joseph is a fruitful bough,
A fruitful bough by a well. . . .
The archers have . . .
Shot at him and hated him.
But his bow remained in strength,
And the arms of his hands were made strong
By the hands of the Mighty God of Jacob.
—GEN. 49:22–24

We have been discussing the valuing the patriarchs in the Old Testament practiced in giving their children the family blessing. Shining threads of love and value are woven through the fabric of a blessing like this one, which Jacob gave his son Joseph. Jacob praised his son's productive and positive life, his strength in overcoming adversity, and his dependence on God. What a powerful expression of love and regard!

We do the same thing when we bless our children, spouse, or friends; we give them a sense of love and self-confidence. We believe this important concept of valuing another person can be found at the heart of every healthy relationship.

We have the power to establish bedrock relationships by focusing on the high value of the other person.

> *Her children rise up and call her blessed;*
> *Her husband also, and he praises her.*
> —PROV. 31:28

Today's verse is from the famous passage about "Superwoman," that virtuous, beautiful, hardworking woman who manages a household, runs a business, looks great, and still has time to sew. "As a result of her industry and accomplishment," the passage seems to say, "her children rise up and call her blessed."

But note that Proverbs doesn't include that phrase, "as a result." So maybe the reverse is true. Maybe the blessing came first! That would certainly fit with our experience of the way the blessing works. Maybe it was *because* her husband and children blessed her with words of appreciation and value that this remarkable woman had the strength and confidence to handle such a productive, busy life.

We honor people who do great things. But the opposite is also true. People are able to do great things because we honor them.

*And the son said to him, "Father, I . . . am no
longer worthy to be called your son." But the father
said . . . "This my son was dead and is alive
again."*

—LUKE 15:21–22,24

We can value people in many ways. We can appreciate their looks, honor their accomplishments, respect their talents, admire their attitudes. Our spoken blessing can appropriately communicate all these forms of regard. But the most healing, most redemptive form of expressing value is based on *relationship*.

This is easy to see in the case of family. I (John) appreciate my wife for many reasons, but I also value her simply because she *is* my wife. I give her a tremendous gift when I bless her for that reason, and not because of what she does for me. The same goes for my children, parents and siblings, friends and church family. And the "relational" circle of blessing widens as we realize God's forgiving and persistent love for all His children. If for no other reason, we must value others and communicate that value simply because we're *all* related on our Father's side!

Father, help me to see you in the face of every person I meet and value that person accordingly.

> *But I say to you, love your enemies, bless those who*
> *curse you, do good to those who hate you, and*
> *pray for those you spitefully use you and persecute*
> *you.*
> —MATT. 5:44

In the Bible, God's statements of blessing often have an "if" attached: they are based on obedience to Him. Repeatedly, God promises blessings on those who remain faithful: "And all these blessings shall come upon you . . . because you obey the voice of the LORD your God" (Deut. 28:2). The New Testament makes a similar requirement: only those having a relationship with God through Jesus will receive God's ultimate blessings.

In other words, God's love is unconditional, but His blessings have a few important strings attached.

However, putting conditions on blessings is God's job, not ours! It's hard not to place higher value on those we love. And it's almost impossible to bless those who curse us! But as we depend on God, He empowers us to value others unconditionally and to leave the "ifs" to Him.

_____

Lord, it's Your job to place conditions on Your blessings. It's my job to obey You and to share Your love with others by attaching high value to them.

*Surely, the smell of my son
is like the smell of a field
which the LORD has blessed.*
—GEN. 27:27

Telling your children that they "smell like a field" would probably not be a compliment! But Jacob knew what his father meant in this blessing. You will, too, if you remember driving through the country when hay or wheat has just been harvested. Particularly with the morning dew on the ground, the smell of a newly cut field can be as refreshing as a mountain spring.

A sentence or two later, Isaac also pictured his son as someone whom other people, including his own family, should greatly respect. He was even someone who deserved to be "bowed down to." Now, in the United States, little premium is placed on bowing. About the only people who know how to bow are orchestra conductors and high school debutantes. In Isaac's day, however, to bow the knee was a mark of respect and honor, something that was expected in the presence of an important person.

These two pictures of praise vividly communicate just how much Isaac valued his son. This message is exactly what modern children (including grown children) need to hear.

Words of value are words we all need to hear.

*And moreover, because the Preacher was wise,
he . . . pondered and sought out and set in order
many proverbs. [He] sought to find acceptable
words. . . .*
—ECCL. 12:9–10

Blessing someone with words of value isn't always
easy. As we have seen, sometimes the perfect time to
pronounce such important words can get lost in a busy
schedule. At other times, stating how much we love
someone can feel awkward, and the recipient may feel
embarrassed about hearing it. And sometimes, direct
expressions of value lose impact because they are
linked to performance: "I think you're great because
you make good grades" . . . or help with chores . . . or
whatever.

But there is a better way to communicate a message
of high value and acceptance, a way to picture a person's good qualities and character traits apart from
performance. Hidden inside the family blessing is a
key to communicating such feelings to our children,
spouse, friends, or church family. We can perfect this
with only a little practice, and even get around the
walls a defensive adult or child can set up. The key is
found in the way word pictures are used throughout
the Scriptures.

*The scriptural practice of using word pictures offers a helpful tool
for communicating value to others.*

. . . We saw the giants . . . and we were like grasshoppers in our own sight. . . .

—NUM. 13:33

One day a friend and I (John) were eating lunch in Dallas, Texas, at a quaint basement restaurant. From our table we could see the stairs leading from street down to the restaurant. At the top of the stairs stood a little girl of about two years old. We also saw two huge tennis shoes and a massive hand clasping her tiny one. Then the shoes started down the stairs, and we could see more of this very large man helping his daughter down the stairs. They reached the foot of the stairs, and we recognized a football player for the Dallas Cowboys. At 6′4″ and 265 pounds, he filled most of the doorway! And as he and his daughter passed our table (the ground shaking and plates rattling), my friend whispered, "Boy, what a moose!"

Calling this man a moose is using a word picture. Randy White does not have antlers and fur, nor does he outweigh even a baby moose. Yet I knew my friend was saying basically the same thing the Hebrew spies to Canaan expressed with a different word picture. We were in the presence of someone very big!

Word pictures communicate meaning vividly and directly.

> *A word fitly spoken is like apples of gold*
> *in settings of silver.*   —PROV. 25:11

We use word pictures all the time, even when we don't realize it.

Have you ever said, "I feel like my head's coming off!" when you had a headache? Or heard someone say, "Their lights are on, but no one's home!"? Both are word pictures!

A junior high school girl who tells her slumber-party friends that her latest boyfriend is a dream does not mean he will evaporate when she wakes up (even if it frequently happens!).

We use so many other pictures throughout the day. Word pictures have become part of the language: "You look like a million bucks." "I feel like death warmed over." "He's as strong as an ox." "She's as pretty as a picture."

Each of these "pictures" expresses an emotion apart from the literal meaning of the words.

What word pictures do you commonly use in the course of a day?

Judah is a lion's whelp. . . .
And as a lion, who shall rouse him? . . .
Naphtali is a deer let loose;
He uses beautiful words.
—GEN. 49:9,21

When Jacob blessed his sons, he used a different word picture with each of them.

Judah, for example, he depicted as a "lion's cub." In the ancient Near East, a lion portrayed strength and was also a symbol of royalty.* This word picture, then, illustrated Judah's leadership qualities and strength of character. Naphtali, on the other hand, was characterized as a deer. The grace and beauty of this gentle animal were used to show the artistic qualities this son possessed. And Joseph, as we have seen, was described as "a fruitful bough by a well" (Gen. 49:22).

Each of Jacob's sons was an individual, and each received a blessing depicting his value to his father in the form of a word picture he could always remember.

Word pictures help make the blessing personal and appropriate.

*J. D. Douglas, *New Bible Dictionary,* "Lion of Judah," (Grand Rapids: Wm. B. Eerdmans Publishing, 1971 edition), p. 742.

The song of songs, which is Solomon's.
—SONG 1:1

The Old Testament patriarchs blessed people with specific word pictures. But before you call your child or spouse a lion, a doe, or a fruitful bough, you might learn more about how word pictures can be used effectively. Let's turn to an Old Testament book that is filled with them.

In the Song of Solomon, God's picture of an ideal courtship and marriage, this loving couple uses word pictures more than eighty times.*

Although Song of Solomon specifically pictures marriage, its use of word pictures can be adapted to any relationship. Over the next few days, we will examine how this couple communicated love, acceptance, and praise. We will discover elements that make word pictures effective to communicate high value.

Read Song of Solomon 1 and note the word pictures. Can you imagine using such pictures yourself?

*Some people question whether Solomon is a suitable model for a godly marriage. We feel his story can be helpful for two reasons. First, he did not take foreign wives and concubines until later in life, and most scholars think this book was written early. Second, *any person* could leave their first love if they stop walking with God, as Solomon did.

Behold, you are fair, my love!
Behold, you are fair!
You have dove's eyes behind your veil.
—SONG 4:1

Let's begin our look at the way word pictures are used in Song of Solomon by taking a look at the young king's wedding night. Not often is someone's wedding night written for posterity, but this one is worth remembering. This is a loving record of a godly relationship. Solomon praises his bride seven times (the biblical number of perfection), stressing that she is altogether beautiful to him. He begins his praise, "You have dove's eyes behind your veil."

With this word picture, Solomon uses an everyday object (a dove) to describe a character trait or physical attribute (his beloved's eyes). The gentle, shy, and tender nature of these creatures would be familiar to his bride. By using a familiar object, Solomon communicates far more meaning with a picture than he could by using mere words. As a bonus, each time she saw a dove thereafter, she would remember how her husband valued her.

Key #1: Effective word pictures are based on familiar objects.

> *A present is a precious stone in the eyes of its possessor; wherever he turns, he prospers.*
>
> —PROV. 17:8

Nancy was born in late December, near Christmas. As she grew, her parents told her how much they valued her by comparing her to a familiar object. "You're God's special Christmas gift to us," they would say. Each Christmas (for thirty-five years now), a small package appears under the Christmas tree. The package is addressed to Nancy's parents from Jesus, but Nancy receives the honor of opening it. Inside, she always finds her baby picture!

Nancy remembers one time this family tradition especially blessed her: "It was my thirtieth birthday, and I was really struggling with growing older. When I was at my lowest point, I received a package in the mail. In the package was a brightly wrapped box, and inside was my baby picture and a note from my parents. It wasn't even Christmas! And being reminded that I was their special 'Christmas gift' filled my heart with love and warmth."

As an exercise, think of someone you love and want to bless. Write down two or three familiar objects you could use to give them the gift of telling how much they mean to you.

> *Your neck is like the tower of David,*
> *built for an armory,*
> *on which hang a thousand bucklers,*
> *all shields of mighty men.*
> —SONG 4:4

Was Solomon trying to end his marriage by comparing his wife's neck to an armored tower? Certainly not.

High above the old city of Jerusalem stood the Tower of David. During peacetime, the war shields of David's "mighty men," the nation's warriors, hung on the tower. A farmer working outside the city walls would find those shields a reassuring sight. But if the shields were down, he would know to dash inside the walls!

Solomon's word picture now makes more sense. In Old Testament times a person's neck stood for his or her appearance *and* attitude. For Solomon, the peace and security represented in David's tower provided a powerful illustration to express his love for his bride. He praised the way she carried herself—with serenity and security.*

Key #2: Effective word pictures match the emotional meaning of the trait you praise with the object you've picked.

*S. Craig Glickman, *A Song for Lovers* (Downers Grove, IL: InterVarsity Press, 1974), p. 48.

> *And as one whom his mother comforts,*
> *so I will comfort you.* —ISA. 66:13

A mother had noticed how helpful and protective her oldest daughter had been with her little brother and sister. The mother decided to find a creative way to communicate words of high value to her daughter. First, she looked around for a familiar object that represented some of those same characteristics (the first key to using word pictures). She saw the family cat, who was attentively nursing her kittens. This mother cat beautifully illustrated the emotional meaning of care and protection (the second key to using word pictures).

Bringing her daughter to see mama cat and her kittens, she said, "Sweetheart, I'm so proud of you. The way you look out for Andrew and Shana reminds me of Mama Kitty." The little girl beamed; she understood exactly what her mother meant. By using a familiar object that conveyed the appropriate emotional meaning, this wise mother gave her daughter a living illustration of her value to her mother.

What familiar pictures like the mother kitty and the mother described in today's Scripture could you choose to convey a message of love and tenderness?

Do not look upon me, because I am dark,
because the sun has tanned me.

—SONG 1:6

Like many young women who might unexpectedly meet a dashing young king, the Shulamite woman who was to become Solomon's bride was insecure about her appearance. When she first met Solomon, she said, "Do not look upon me, because I am dark." But after she had been around Solomon for only a short time, she called herself, "the rose of Sharon" (2:1). Quite a change of perspective!

If Solomon had simply said, "You're cute," his beloved's insecurity could have found a dozen reasons why this matter-of-fact statement could not be true: "Maybe his eyesight is bad" or "Maybe my father paid him to say that." Insecure people today often use similar reasoning to shrug off compliments. But word pictures have the power to capture people's attention in spite of our insecurities. For some reason, we will listen to praise more intently when it is packaged in a word picture.

Key #3: Effective word pictures can penetrate defensiveness and overcome insecurity.

> *I am my beloved's,*
> *and his desire is toward me.*
> —SONG 7:10

How do we know Solomon's word pictures really got through to his insecure bride? Look at how her attitude changed over the course of their married life.

During their courtship, she viewed their relationship with a certain insecurity and possessiveness, as evidenced by her statement: "My beloved is mine, and I am his" (2:16). But as their story continues after their wedding, and as she grows more secure in his love, watch the subtle but powerful change in how she views their relationship. She tells the ladies of the court, "I am my beloved's, and my beloved is mine" (6:3). Then, as their story draws to a close, she even says, "I am my beloved's, and his desire is toward me." This final statement shows a lot more security than her view of their relationship just before their wedding night. Why? Solomon's word pictures of praise and great value (more than fifty of them!) helped build security in an insecure woman's heart.

Do you know someone whose insecurities make it hard for him or her to accept praise? Try to think of a word picture that could help that person hear what you want to say.

Then He spoke many things to them in parables.
—MATT. 13:3

A word picture's ability to overcome insecurity is surely one reason our Lord used parables to communicate. These extended object lessons, rich in word pictures, kept his audience's attention, even if they had a hard time hearing His message.

Jesus knew the importance of using word pictures with those who were timid. He would talk about being the Good Shepherd who watched over the flock; the true vine that could bring spiritual sustenance; and the bread of life that would provide spiritual nourishment. By using everyday objects, He was able to penetrate the walls of insecurity and mistrust these people had built. Word pictures hold a key to our hearts that simple words do not.

———————

Why do you think that word pictures are easier to hear than plain words?

> *Woe to you, scribes and Pharisees, hypocrites! For*
> *you are like whitewashed tombs which indeed*
> *appear beautiful outwardly, but inside are full of*
> *dead men's bones and all uncleanness.*
> —MATT. 23:27

Word pictures can also be used effectively with people who are defensive when we want to talk with them. Something about a story or a picture compels even angry, stubborn people to listen when they don't want to.

Jesus was a master at using word pictures to speak to defensive people like the Pharisees who really didn't want to hear what He was saying! Today's scripture is a powerful example. True, it isn't used to express high value—except in the sense that Jesus valued the Pharisees enough to try to get through to them. But the vividness of the example illustrates how powerful a word picture can be. And from all indications, it worked. Would the Pharisees have lobbied against Jesus if He had not gotten under their skin?

Can you think of a time when defensiveness hampered your communication with another person? How would using a word picture have helped you get through?

Like a lily among thorns,
so is my love among the daughters. . . .
My beloved is like a . . . young stag.
—SONG 2:2,9

Arms crossed, eyes angry, Bill and Barb sat in the counseling office and argued with the angry words threatening their marriage. Bill, who loved the rugged outdoors, had moved his family far from any towns. Barb, born and raised in the city, resented being isolated from her friends and left alone with two toddlers while Bill went hunting or fishing.

I (Gary) said, "Bill, I see you as a powerful oil painting of a mighty stag standing proudly near a mountain stream. Your heavy frame is carved of weathered wood. Barb, you're a lovely floral watercolor with dazzling hues and fine brush strokes, set off with an oval mat and a narrow, elegant frame. Now, both of you are beautiful pictures, even though you look so different. But you are both so busy trying to repaint the other's picture that you don't see the beauty."

That word picture communicated volumes to this couple. Over the next few weeks, instead of trying to change each other, they tried to look for the beauty in each other. When they did, they began to rediscover the attraction that had originally drawn them together.

Using word pictures can overcome barriers of anger and rekindle affection.

> *New things I declare;*
> *Before they spring forth I tell you of them.*
> —ISA. 42:9

Word pictures effectively offer a route around conversational ruts that prevent us from really hearing each other. One woman told us how this happened in her life:

> Stan [not his real name] and I have many discussions about the same subjects. A person could record the conversation and play it over and over. Then, about two weeks ago, I painted a word picture to show him how I felt about his supporting me in front of his family . . . . I read it to him myself so he could hear the emphasis. It worked! I had his attention. We had one of our most meaningful talks ever.

What conversational ruts hamper communication in your own relationships? Would a word picture create a successful detour to help you bless someone or communicate honestly?

Blessed are you, Simon Bar-Jonah. . . . And I also say to you that you are Peter.

—MATT. 16:17–18

This powerful moment of Jesus' ministry illustrates another reason word pictures can so effectively bless someone. A word picture illustrates a person's undeveloped traits and thus motivates that person to grow and improve.

Jesus did this when He changed Simon's name to Peter, which in Greek means "rock." At that time, Peter certainly didn't act like a rock of strength and stability. And he certainly wasn't very rock-like when he tried to talk Jesus out of facing the cross, or when he fell asleep in the garden, or when he denied Jesus three times. Even after the Resurrection, when Peter and Jesus walked together on the shore, Peter displayed some very shaky characteristics. Jesus was mapping out Peter's future, but Peter was just concerned about what *John* would do.

But Jesus saw the potential in this rough fisherman. He used a word picture to plant in Peter's heart a vision of the man he could become. In the Book of Acts, we read the exciting story about the rock Peter did become.

Key #4: Word pictures point out a person's potential.

This I recall to my mind,
therefore I have hope.
—LAM. 3:21

The unthinkable had happened to her. Her husband had deserted her to pursue an immoral relationship. With two toddlers and no marketable skills, she faced relentless struggles. But now, six years later, she has a good job that lets her spend time with her children and still provide their basic financial needs.

When we asked what was her greatest source of help during those first years, she said: "The Lord, certainly. But from a human perspective, I have to point to my father. Every time I wanted to quit school or give up, he would say, 'You'll make it, Jenny. You're my rock of Gibraltar. I know you'll make it.' I didn't feel like a rock. My whole world seemed to avalanche. But knowing he pictured me that way helped. It gave me the hope that maybe I could make it."

We can give this same hope to others when we use a word picture to describe their abilities—especially abilities they might not acknowledge or recognize.

How can you use word pictures to give hope to those who are struggling?

Listen, for I will speak of excellent things,
and from the opening of my lips will come right things.
—PROV. 8:6

We have discussed four keys which make word pictures effective in communicating high value:

1. Word pictures use a familiar object to communicate meaning.
2. Word pictures match the emotional meaning of the trait you are praising.
3. Word pictures overcome insecurities and unravel defenses.
4. Word pictures can highlight a person's potential.

The adage tells us one picture is worth a thousand words. When we link a word picture with a message of high value, we multiply our message a thousand times.

As an exercise, pick three names from your list of people you want to bless. Think of two different word pictures that describe the way you value each of these people. Write down these pictures and share them over the next few weeks.

> *Where is God my Maker,*
> *who gives songs in the night?*
> —JOB 35:10

Has our talk of word pictures left you convinced but frustrated, feeling you're "just not creative"? If so, relax! First, it's not the only way to communicate high value. But second, you may be surprised at how creative you can be, with God's help. One woman wrote to us:

> After I finished reading about word pictures, I thought how neat it would be to have an imagination like that. I did not think I had an imagination, but God sure does. I prayed one day that He would show me a picture to express how my family makes me feel about my relationship and my walk with Him. About a week later, He gave me a word picture. I repeated it to myself and then told my prayer partner, who loved it. I typed it out, proofreading it several times and adding to it each time I read through it. . . . It hasn't changed anyone yet, but I have faith in God to wait for His timing, not mine.

God is the source of all good gifts, including songs in the night and effective word pictures.

Even a child is known by his deeds.
—PROV. 20:11

It's Saturday morning. For once, Dad is home instead of catching up at the office. He's just settled down to enjoy the paper when his eight-year-old son sidles up and stands by the chair. Dad doesn't want to be interrupted, so he keeps reading. The son doesn't leave. Finally, realizing the boy won't go away, the father slams down the paper. "All right," he grumpily asks, "What do you want?"

"Daddy, I have something for you. Hold out your hand." Into the dad's outstretched hand drops a bunch of wadded dollar bills and some change. Confused, the dad asks, "What is this?"

The son proudly answers, "This is eight dollars and fifty-four cents. It's all I've got. And Daddy, I'll give it all to you if you'll just stay home and play with me today."

That child, and every child, is begging, "Please bless me. I know your work is important. I know your relaxation is important. But am I important? Show me."

Words of value can truly change a life—but we are known by our deeds as well as by our words. We show our loved ones they are valuable by giving them our time and attention.

> *A prophet is not without honor except in his own country and in his own house.*
> —MATT. 13:57

In this verse, Jesus referred to the fact that His own family and townspeople seemed to have difficulty understanding who He was. That's not surprising. Sometimes we all have trouble really "seeing" the people we love. Because they are so familiar, and because of the irritations that come with closeness, we sometimes undervalue those we should cherish most.

Attaching high value to the people we love, therefore, may require a conscious effort to see them with new eyes. Seeing them in a new setting may help: volunteer at a child's school; help them with a new activity; visit a friend at work. Dressing up and going on a date (or meeting for lunch) may help you see your mate in a different context; attending a professional meeting or conference may be even more effective.

Pray for the grace to see the ones closest to you with new eyes so you can bless them more effectively.

*Now may the Lord of peace Himself give you peace
always in every way.* —2 THESS. 3:16

Note how each of these acts of everyday blessing communicates a clear message of high value.

1. My mother and father would ask us children our opinions on important family decisions.

2. When my father faced a work transfer, he changed jobs so I could finish my senior year at the same school.

3. My mom had a great sense of humor, but never made us kids the brunt of her jokes.

4. My parents didn't change things in my bedroom without asking me first.

5. My folks pursued resolving conflict with me instead of letting issues build.

6. When I wrecked my parents' car, my father's first reaction was to hug me and let me cry.

7. My dad corrected me without getting angry or lecturing me.

8. My parents were patient when I went through my long hair stage in high school.

May you feel God's peace as you continue weaving blessing into your daily life.

> *Rise up, my love, my fair one,*
> *and come away.*
> *For lo, the winter is past,*
> *the rain is over and gone.*
> *The flowers appear on the earth;*
> *the time of singing has come.*
> —SONG 2:10–12

Today, take a break to praise God for the beauty and promise of spring. If you can, take a walk to see what is blooming or stretching up through the ground. Take a hint from the old hymn and "count your blessings."

What if you're facing a difficult time and your list of blessings seems small? Confess your pain to Him (even if you've done so a million times already) and thank Him for His promises of blessing. Even if you can't feel it, God is working to redeem your pain and make you a blessing to others. Just for today, resolve to rest in Him and enjoy the blessings of springtime.

Come to the Lord today with a heart of thanksgiving and hope.
Praise Him for the blessings He has given you, and thank Him that
you have the opportunity to bless others.

> *"May God Almighty bless you,*
> *and make you fruitful and multiply you . . .*
> *and give you the blessing of Abraham,*
> *to you and your descendants with you,*
> *that you may inherit the land*
> *in which you are a stranger.*
> —GEN. 28:3–4

These words, which Isaac spoke before Jacob went to live with his uncle, beautifully illustrate yet another facet of the Old Testament blessing. This future-oriented blessing commits loved ones to God's care and says, "May the Lord design for you a beautiful future."

But the Old Testament blessings were more than vague best wishes for the future. As this one shows, they specifically painted a vivid, personalized picture of a hopeful tomorrow. And this picture of tomorrow is also an important element in the blessing today.

When we picture a positive future for our children, a spouse, or friends, we help bring out the best in their lives by giving them a positive direction to strive toward. We also surround them with hope.

The fourth vital element of the blessing is to picture a special future for the ones we bless.

> *You are Peter, and on this rock I will build My
> church, and the gates of Hades shall not prevail
> against it.*
> —MATT. 16:18

When Jesus gave Simon the name "Peter," which
means rock, He did more than use a word picture to
show Peter's value. He also pictured a breathtaking future for His disciple. We can do the same for those we
love by suggesting a bright tomorrow for them.

"God has given you such a sensitive heart. I
wouldn't be surprised if you help many people when
you grow up."

"You have a wonderful imagination. You could be a
great artist or writer."

"You have a real gift for relating to children. I just
know you'll be a wonderful teacher."

"I'm impressed by your work and by your people
skills. If you wanted to, you could probably be head of
this organization someday."

When children—and adults—hear words like these,
which picture a special future for them, they begin to
move toward that future.

*Can you remember a time when someone pictured a positive future
for you? How have those words affected your life?*

*Your word is a lamp to my feet
and a light to my path.*
—PS. 119:105

Have you ever camped in the woods on a dark night? If so, you probably remember what it's like to walk away from your campfire into the night. In only a few steps, darkness can seem to swallow you. Turning and walking back toward the fire is much more reassuring than groping around in the dark. And having a flashlight for the pathway is even better.

Today's Scripture compares God's Word to a campfire or a flashlight on a dark night. Human words picturing a special future have a similar potential. They can draw a person toward the warmth of genuine concern and fulfilled potential. And instead of leaving that person to walk into a dark unknown, they can illuminate a pathway lined with hope and purpose.

When we picture a special future for our children, a spouse, or friends, we provide them with a clear light to help illuminate their path in life.

Hope deferred makes the heart sick,
but when the desire comes, it is a tree of life.
—PROV. 13:12

Why does picturing a special future for our loved ones provide so much power in shaping their lives? One reason is because humans simply were not designed to live without hope—and picturing a special future is one way of planting hope deep in a person's heart.

But hopelessness is not just a "heart matter." The body and mind are also affected. Most of us have experienced catching a bad cold during a time of extreme discouragement. Most of us have heard of medical cases in which the patient "just gave up." Most of us have read stories about suicide notes stating, "I'm sorry. I just couldn't face one more day."

But the invigorating opposite is also true. Hope can pull us through the most difficult times. It can make us "hold on" in illness and rally our resources to fight battles. Hope, instilled by those who care enough to picture a special blessing, really can truly be "a tree of life."

When we portray a special future for other people, we plant life-giving hope within their hearts.

Reuben, you are my firstborn. . . .
Unstable as water, you shall not excel.
—GEN. 49:3–4

Being told the future is hopeful and something to anticipate can greatly affect a person's attitude. Unfortunately, the opposite is also true.

"You'd better hope you can find someone who will take care of you when you're older. You're so irresponsible you'll never be able to do anything for yourself."

"Why bother to study? You'll just get married and drop out of school."

"You're just like your father—lazy. You'll never amount to anything."

What a way to short-circuit someone's future! If children hear only words predicting relationship problems or personal inadequacies, they can turn and travel down the destructive path pictured for them.

Why would a person say degrading words like these? Meditate on some of the causes—anger, fear of spoiling, carelessness, habit—that might lead you to make similar hopeless predictions for someone.

I have heard the rebuke that reproaches me.
—JOB 20:3

How could anyone as dumb and ugly as you have such a beautiful child?" Mark's mother grinned as she cuddled her grandson. Most observers would have brushed her words aside as a bad joke, but they brought tears to Mark's eyes.

"Stop!" Mark shouted. "That's all I've ever heard from you. It's taken years for me to believe I'm not ugly and dumb. Why do you think I haven't been home for so long? Don't ever call me dumb again!"

Mark's mother was stunned. She had meant her words as a joke. And she had always kidded her children like that—just as her mother had kidded her. But she didn't really mean what she said. Surely her children knew that!

When it concerns predictions about their personalities or futures, children are literalists—especially when the predictions come from their parents, the most important people in their lives. Regardless of our intentions, they take to heart any words that reproach them.

What man is there among you who, if his son asks for bread, will give him a stone? Or if he asks for a fish, will he give him a serpent? —MATT. 7:9–10

Through the years, Mark's mother repeatedly gave her children negative pictures of their future. She was jesting, but the results were far from funny!

"Nobody will want to date a fat mess like you!" she would say with a resounding laugh—and her daughter would ache inside. Unfortunately, her jokes became self-fulfilling prophecies. Discouraged, the girl neglected her appearance to the point that boys really were uninterested.

"You might as well drop geometry now; that's for smart kids," she would remark. Her youngest would throw down his pencil and quit trying to understand the math problem. Eventually, after flunking his junior year, he dropped out of high school.

Mark took the opposite approach. He became the family "overachiever." His lifestyle bordered on extreme workaholism in his need to be successful. He strived to achieve to prove to his mother that her predictions were wrong.

Picturing a negative future for children is like giving them a stone or a serpent.

This is my comfort in my affliction,
For Your word has given me life.
—PS. 119:50

We met the man when we appeared on his radio talk show in the Midwest. Having never met this dynamic radio personality, we had no idea he had been a paraplegic since birth. His story dramatically illustrates the power of picturing a special future for a child.

"My junior high years," he said, "were the most insecure time of my life. I had acne. I was in a wheelchair. I didn't know what God was going to do with me, and had no idea He could ever use me. I even thought about killing myself . . . but I was afraid it would hurt. Then two men in a church came to me at different times and said, 'You have a great voice. I wouldn't be surprised if God ended up using your voice to serve him'."

What does that man do today? Christian radio. A light went on in his heart when those two men cared enough to "give him life" by picturing a special future for him.

Portraying a special future can rescue a hurting person from despair and point them in an optimistic direction. Do you know someone who faces extra challenges and could use a word of hope?

So they sent away Rebekah their sister and her nurse, and Abraham's servant and his men. And they blessed Rebekah and said to her:

> *"Our sister, may you become*
> *the mother of thousands of ten thousands;*
> *and may your descendants possess*
> *the gates of those who hate them.'"*
> —GEN. 24:59–60

Old Testament blessings gave rich promises for the future. We can see this by looking at the words of blessing Rebekah's brother and mother pronounced before she left to be Isaac's wife.

At the time this blessing was given, Rebekah was not married. She certainly had no children. Yet this picture of a fruitful future was a powerful gift. The picture gave her the security of knowing she had something to anticipate. Surely these words must have echoed in her mind and given her hope as she struggled with infertility and then puzzled over why her unborn twins seemed to struggle together in her womb. Could these words have influenced her to play such an active role in determining the future of her sons?

The blessing in the Scriptures puts a high priority on providing a special future for each child.

> The LORD shall preserve your going out and your
> coming in from this time forth, and even
> forevermore.
> —PS. 121:8

Final exams. End of school festivities. The promise of summer. Graduation. A new job.

For anyone in school or anyone who has attended school—which includes most of us—May is a time of milestones and transitions, of major "goings out" and "comings in." These special times provide golden opportunities to bless people we know.

Marking a rite of passage with a suitable blessing is a very old tradition. The patriarchs' blessings were specifically tailored to fit important milestones in the family's life: the birth of a child, the child's coming of age, a betrothal or marriage, a farewell, a deathbed. The custom of marking special transitions with a blessing continues today in Orthodox Jewish families, as well as in many Christian families and churches. This custom is well worth preserving or reviving.

What rites of passage or major transitions will your family or church experience soon—graduation, new driver's licenses, new babies, new jobs? Make each milestone an opportunity to picture a special future for those you love.

The fear of the LORD is the beginning of knowledge.
—PROV. 1:7

This blessing based on Proverbs 1 pictures a future of wisdom and understanding. What a wonderful graduation blessing this would make!

O Lord, may _____[insert person's name]_____ come to know Your wisdom and instruction. May _____[person's name]_____ discern the sayings of understanding. May [he/she] receive the instruction in wise behavior, righteousness, justice, and equity. May You, Lord, give this precious one prudence, knowledge, and discretion. May [he/she] truly listen and increase in learning, always seeking wise counsel. May _____[person's name]_____ understand the greatest of all Your instructions—to love and value You with all [his/her] heart. Then will [he/she] begin to find knowledge.

Read this blessing first with your name in the blank. Pray for a future of "wise behavior, righteousness, justice," but especially pray that you will come to love God more.

Judah, you are he whom your brothers shall praise;
your hand shall be on the neck of your enemies;
your father's children shall bow down before you.
—GEN. 49:8

As we have seen, Jacob received a blessing that pictured a special future for him: "Let the peoples serve you and nations bow down to you." Then Jacob passed this part of the blessing to his firstborn, Judah. The blessing pictured a special future that would take years to become reality, but offered Judah hope as each year unfolded.

As we noted earlier, these patriarchs' words held a prophetic nature that is not part of the blessing today. We parents cannot predict our children's futures with biblical accuracy, but we can provide them with the hope and direction. As our children begin to live up to these goals, they will gain added security in an insecure world.

The picture of the future we give through the blessing can give our children an advantage.

I have taught you in the way of wisdom;
I have led you in right paths.

—PROV. 4:11

Orthodox Jewish communities constantly use wishes for a special future as tools for leading children (and adults) "in the right paths." At synagogue, for instance, the rabbi often tells young boys:

> May this little child grow to manhood. Even as he has entered into the Covenant, so may he enter into the study of Torah, into the wedding-canopy and into a life of good deeds.*

This synagogue blessing offers a helpful model for blessings picturing the future. For instance, I (John), could bless my daughter, Laura, this way:

> May this little child grow to womanhood. Even as she has been dedicated to the Lord, so may she drink deep of God's holy Word, grow into healthy relationships, and make a positive difference in her world.

Write your own version of a synagogue blessing for a child you know.

*M. J. Cohen, *The Jewish Celebration Book* (Philadelphia: The Jewish Publication Society of America, 1946), p. 108.

You shall keep them, O Lord,
You shall preserve them from this generation forever.
—PS. 12:7

We were once invited to visit an Orthodox Jewish home on Thanksgiving. Forty people—three generations—gathered for the meal. But before it was served, the grandfather gathered the family. He then went around, placing his hands on the head of every person in the room, saying to each man, "May God richly bless you, and may He make you as Ephraim and Manasseh" and to each woman, "May God richly bless you, and may you grow to be like Rebekah and Sarah." From the oldest child to the youngest grandchild, this time of blessing pictured a special future for each person in the room. Far from being a meaningless ritual, it provided everyone with a warm wish for a fulfilling life.

Future-oriented words extend the blessing from generation to generation.

*For I know the thoughts that I think toward you,
says the LORD, thoughts of peace and not of evil, to
give you a future and a hope.* —JER. 29:11

Picturing a positive future is a vital part of our blessing from the Lord. Look at the beautiful way the
prophet Jeremiah assures us of our special future in
our relationship with the Lord. Repeatedly, the Bible
spells out the "future and hope" God has in mind for
His people. We also see His faithfulness in making that
future a reality.

"I will make you a great nation," God promised
Abraham and His descendants (Gen. 12:2). He did.

"I will deliver you from Egypt and bring you to a
Promised Land," He told Moses (see Ex. 3:8). He did
that, too.

"I will bring you out of your captivity in Babylon,"
He comforted His captive people (see Jer. 29:14). He
kept that promise.

Best of all, God promised the people of Israel a Savior: "'Behold, the virgin shall be with child, and bear
a Son, and they shall call His name Immanuel,' which
is translated, 'God with us.'" (Matt. 1:23). And once
again, to our great joy, He did it!

*How would your life and relationships change if you really took to
heart God's blessing and promises of a special future?*

> *In My Father's house are many mansions. . . . I go*
> *to prepare a place for you. And if I go and prepare*
> *a place for you, I will come again and receive you*
> *to Myself; that where I am, there you may be also."*
> —JOHN 14:2–3

God's promises of a special future reached their peak in Jesus, but they didn't stop there. In fact, Jesus went to great lengths to assure His insecure disciples of a special future with Him. During their last Passover meal together, Jesus made sure they knew their time together would not end at His death.

Even after Jesus ascended into heaven, God made sure His followers were reassured of this. Again and again, through the writers of the Acts, the Epistles, and the Revelation, He assures us of the "future and the hope" we have in Him. And the New Testament ends with a vivid and wonderful description of the gigantic party awaiting us at the end of time: "Blessed are those who are called to the marriage supper of the Lamb!" (Rev. 19:9). No wonder the apostle John closed His Book of Revelation with these eager words in Revelation 22:20, "Even so, come, Lord Jesus!"

As followers of Christ, our ultimate special future is with Him.

*Therefore do not worry about tomorrow, for
tomorrow will worry about its own things.*
—MATT. 6:34

At first, this verse might seem to warn against the
kind of future orientation we have been describing. So
would James's caution: "Come now, you who say,
'. . . tomorrow we will go to such and such a city, spend
a year there, buy and sell, and make a profit'; whereas
you do not know what will happen tomorrow. . . . Instead you ought to say, 'If the Lord wills, we shall live
and do this or that'" (James 4:13–15).

But we really don't face a contradiction. Jesus and
James caution us against worry and smug denial, not
confident hope. Besides, what better guarantee
against anxiety and defensive arrogance than the gentle assurance that we are loved and valued and that
our hope for the future is real!

---

*Jesus and James tell us not to worry and not to presume. But our
confidence in a special future—either in our lifetime or afterward—
enables us to live a worry-free, trusting life.*

> *Blessed are you who trust in the LORD,*
> *and whose hope is the LORD.*
> *For you shall be like a tree planted by the waters,*
> *which spreads out its roots by the river,*
> *and will not fear when heat comes;*
> *but its leaf will be green,*
> *and will not be anxious in the year of drought,*
> *nor will cease from yielding fruit.*
> —JER. 17:7–8 (adapted)

This blessing comes straight from Jeremiah to you—adapted only slightly to bring its hope-filled message closer to home. These verses picture a wonderful future of beauty and growth for those who trust in the Lord. But this lovely promise also has a flip side. The same passage describing these blessings also pictures a curse for those who choose to rely on themselves:

> *Cursed is the man who trusts in man*
> *and makes flesh his strength,*
> *whose heart departs from the LORD.*
> *For he shall be like a shrub in the desert,*
> *and shall not see when good comes,*
> *but shall inhabit the parched places in the wilderness,*
> *in a salt land which is not inhabited (vv. 5–6).*

God promises a special future for us if we trust in Him.

Be transformed by the renewing of your mind, that you may prove what is that good and acceptable and perfect will of God.
—ROM. 12:2 (emphasis added)

The written Word is not the only means through which God communicates His message of blessing. Many physical pictures in nature illustrate the importance of providing a special future for those we love. Anyone who has ever watched a butterfly emerge from its cocoon has seen such a picture. The caterpillar is probably not on anyone's list of the world's "ten most beautiful creatures." Yet a caterpillar can potentially be transformed into a gorgeous butterfly.

What does this have to do with the blessing? Words picturing a special future for a child, spouse, or friend can be agents of transformation in their lives. Spoken blessings really do have that transforming power. In fact, the actual Greek term for the transformation of caterpillar to butterfly is the word Paul used in today's scripture.

Pray that your words of blessing can help transform someone's life.

> *Be transformed by the renewing of your mind, that*
> *you may prove what is that good and acceptable*
> *and perfect will of God.*
> —ROM. 12:2 (emphasis added)

What does it mean to be "transformed by the renewing of your mind"? One New Testament commentator explains the concept, "Since men are transformed by the action of the mind, transformed by what they think, how important to have the organ of thought renewed!"*

In other words, godly thoughts and thinking patterns can transform us into godly men or women, rather than leaving us to be squeezed into the imperfect mold of the world.

Let's see how this works with regard to the blessing. Children have the potential to be all God intends them to be. During the years we have children at home, the words we speak can wrap around them like a cocoon. What we say shapes and develops their perceptions and thinking patterns. Loving words help children change and develop in a positive direction.

We renew our minds and the minds of those we love by wrapping them in loving words and hope-filled visions.

*Jay Stifler, *The Epistle to the Romans* (Chicago: Moody Press, 1983), p. 119.

Many of the saints I shut up in prison.
—ACTS 26:10

Our words can promote growth by wrapping others in a cocoon of love and hope. But some words that wrap around people restrict growth—imprisoning their spirits in tight cocoons that twist their self-confidence and warp their futures.

"You're a bum. You'll always be a bum," Barry's father said to him as he left for his college graduation. Those were familiar words. In fact, until his father's death, they were the only comments Barry received about his future. Unconsciously, Barry tried to live up to those words. When we first saw him, he had just lost an important position in a major insurance company. Though intelligent and talented, Barry lost all motivation after he was hired. He would handle projects and people irresponsibly. Within six months, he was out looking for yet another job. Those three words: "You're a bum," replayed in Barry's mind and surrounded him, trapping him in a negative cocoon. He emerged insecure, irresponsible, and defeated.

Eventually, the words that wrap around us will shape our futures.

> *And now, Lord, what do I wait for?*
> *My hope is in You.* —PS. 39:7

Let's look at another important nature picture that mirrors what happens when we bless our children with a special future. Imagine a typical cell in your body. Receptor points are attached around the outside of this cell. To make this easier to understand, let's picture these receptor sites as little people.

Now, floating around near the cell are hormones and enzymes seeking to "shake hands" with (or activate) these receptors. Some body chemicals have the ability to energize a cell's activity. Imagine someone shaking your hand so vigorously that your whole body shakes! That's what happens when certain hormones "shake hands" with a cell receptor. The stimulation, called "positive cooperativity," not only shakes this one receptor site (and makes it work harder as a result); all the other receptor sites nearby also start shaking and working harder!

Words of blessing that picture a positive future act like these positive hormones that attach themselves to a cell. They stimulate positive feelings and decisions that will help a person grow and develop.

Our bones are dry, our hope is lost.
—EZEK. 37:11

Yesterday, we used the picture of a body cell to illustrate what happens when we bless children. Like hormones that "shake hands" with cell receptors and stimulate them positively, words picturing a special future stimulate positive feelings and actions. A child who receives such a gift can have the confidence to develop a talent, run for a school office, or even share his or her faith with other children.

But the reverse is true as well. To continue the cell analogy, not all hormones and enzymes affect receptor sites positively. Has anyone ever squeezed your hand so hard that you almost crumpled over in pain? That's similar to what happens when negative hormones and enzymes grasp a receptor site; it's called negative cooperativity. Not only does the affected receptor site stop working, but all the surrounding receptor sites stop.

Just like the negative hormones that stifle cell activity, a critical picture of the future can stunt healthy growth emotionally, physically, and even spiritually.

> *Why do you not understand My speech? . . . And if*
> *I tell the truth, why do you not believe Me?*
> —JOHN 8:43,46

Jesus spoke these words to the Pharisees. But sometimes you may feel this way when you try to picture a special future for others. Words of blessing can be hard to hear—and it's usually not a matter of your having laryngitis! Sometimes, of course, this "hearing loss" has little to do with us. For example, a friend with a low self-esteem may not "hear" when we point out that she is extremely bright and would succeed in graduate school. But our actions can also influence the way others hear our blessings. Actions don't necessarily speak louder than words—we need the words too. But actions can easily rob our words of their power.

Can you think of a time in your life when somebody's past actions made it difficult for you to hear their words—or have your actions ever made your family and friends hard of hearing? What do you think is the key to avoiding this problem?

For He spoke, and it was done;
He commanded, and it stood fast.
—PS. 33:9

Inconsistent actions are prime culprits in making a blessing hard to hear. If we seriously want to give a message of a special future to our children, we must follow the Lord's example. His faithfulness and consistency act like solid footings on which words of a special future can stand.

Throughout Scripture, the basis for believing God's Word in the future lies in His consistency in fulfilling His word in the past. In the words of another Psalm, we are reminded of the Lord's "marvelous works which He has done, His wonders, and the judgments of His mouth" (Ps. 105:5).

Because God has been reliable in the past, we can believe His words now. The same principle is true in our desire to provide a special future for those we wish to bless. Our past credibility, or lack of it, will directly affect how our words are received now.

Consistency in the past is the first crucial element necessary in making our blessings easy to hear.

Help, LORD . . .
for the faithful disappear from among the sons of men.
—PS. 12:1

Ted's sales job kept him on the road thirty-one weeks each year. When he did come home, he was usually exhausted. This situation undermined his ability to bless his children. Although Ted did well at "picturing" a special future for his children, he rarely followed through on his word.

For instance, when he noticed his daughter's love for animals, Ted promised, "Samantha, we're going to get a horse for you to ride and care for. You might even become a veterinarian someday."

He told his athletic young son, "Bobby, you're pro shortstop material. After I rest, I'll hit you some grounders."

But in a few days he would be gone again, with no more talk of pony or baseball.

Ted finally realized what was happening. He took a cut in pay to get a non-traveling position and tried to make up for his empty promises. But by then Samantha had lost interest in horses, and Bobby didn't have time for baseball. Ted's children had their own friends, interests, and a deep-set impression that their future would not include their father's involvement.

Remember, inconsistent "quality" time cannot make up for consistency in our relationships. Without daily demonstrations of commitment, our pictures of a special future carry as much weight as the air used to speak them.

> *If we confess our sins, He is faithful and just to forgive us our sins and to cleans us from all unrighteousness.*
>
> —1 JOHN 1:9

Yesterday we looked at Ted, whose inconsistency undermined his effectiveness. But Ted's story has a happy ending. Ted truly loved his family and persevered in regaining the ground he had lost. Finally, two years later, Ted had built a "past" with his children that assured them of his best wishes for their future. Samantha even began to rekindle an interest in animals, and Bobby dug his baseball glove out of the bottom of the closet.

Perhaps your past has been anything but consistent with those you want to bless. Today really *is* the first day of the rest of your life. By honoring your commitments today, you can build the "past" upon which words of a special future need to rest.

What circumstances make it difficult for you to act consistently? What changes would make your words of blessing more trustworthy?

*This hope we have as an anchor of the soul, both
sure and steadfast.*
—HEB. 6:19

Here are more examples of ways in which parents
can extend everyday blessings to their children. Do
any of them fit you?

1. My mother tried hard to keep her promises to
   me.
2. My dad would often ask, "What would it take
   for this to be a great year for you?" Then he'd
   try to make it a great year.
3. Even though dad played football in college, he
   never forced me to go out for sports when I
   didn't want to.
4. At least once a year around my birthday, my
   dad would take me out of school for a special
   lunch.
5. My parents frequently told me I was a good
   friend to have.
6. Even when I was in high school, my father
   would sometimes tuck me into bed, just as he
   did when I was little.
7. My mother prayed with me about important
   decisions I faced or even that I would have a
   good day at school.

*The everyday blessings we give to those we love help provide the
hope that anchors their souls.*

Entreat me not to leave you,
Or to turn back from following after you.
—RUTH 1:16

For our words of a special future to take root and grow, we must demonstrate the kind of commitment Ruth expressed to Naomi. This is the commitment to remain in a relationship with a person, supporting that one's growth. Children, especially, need the certainty that we will be around long enough to see our predictions come to pass.

I (Gary) realized this one night at the dinner table when my college-aged daughter suddenly asked her mom, "Do you think you and Dad will ever divorce?" Norma nearly choked. "Kari!" she replied, "You know I would never divorce your dad." Then thinking about it a bit more, Norma added with a twinkle, "Murder maybe, but never divorce!"

After we stopped laughing, we discovered why Kari had asked the question. She was two months into the school year, and already the parents of two classmates had divorced. That night, Kari was asking the same thing every child asks (out loud or silently): "Will you be here in the future as I grow up, or will one of you leave me?"

Commitment is the second crucial element in making our words of blessing easy to hear.

Oh, do not forsake me utterly!
—PS. 119:8

W hat bothers you most about your parents' arguing?" I (John) asked a six-year-old girl during a family counseling session. Her insightful answer surprised us all. Her greatest pain and insecurity weren't caused by the loud voices or the harsh words, but from the fact that "every time my daddy gets mad at my mom, he takes off his wedding ring and throws it away."

Her father said it was "no big deal," but his habit of pulling off his wedding ring and throwing it sent a clear message to his daughter. Every time he "threw away" his wedding ring, this little girl saw her future with her parents (her greatest source of security) sail right along with it. Words of a special future for a child can dissolve into ashes when a husband or wife walks out on a relationship.

Whether you are married or single, a parent or a concerned friend, this story can speak to you. If you want a child to hear your words of a special future, reassure the child that your commitment to him or her will remain strong no matter what happens.

When you walk, your steps will not be hindered,
and when you run, you will not stumble.
—PROV. 4:12

Marcia struggled in school, and eventually her teacher put her in the "slow learners" group. But this did not keep Marcia's parents from picturing a special future for her. Rather than pushing Marcia to "hurry up," her parents praised her for staying with an assignment until its completion. They also noticed that Marcia could explain things clearly to younger children. When Marcia announced that she wanted to be a teacher, they looked beyond her sagging test scores and said, "If you work hard, we know you can be a wonderful teacher!"

With help from tutors and special classes, Marcia struggled through school. She took six and one-half years to finish a four-year college program. But finally, on a beautiful May afternoon, Marcia graduated with an elementary education degree—and a job! Because of her fine job in student teaching, her principal had invited her to return. By encouraging their daughter's dream and picturing a special future for her, Marcia's parents helped turn a "slow learner" into a high achiever.

Picturing a special future can help remove hindrances and stumbling blocks even from a difficult path.

> *The righteousness of the righteous shall be upon himself, and the wickedness of the wicked shall be upon himself.*
> —EZEK. 18:20

Picturing a special picture for others is *not* the same as imposing a future on them or pushing them in a direction they don't really want to go. Parents, especially, may fall into this trap. They love their children and sincerely want God's best. However, their view of "God's best" is colored by their own hopes and fears. A father longs for his son to be an athlete. A single mother desperately wants her daughter to marry and not "have to work."

Parents aren't the only culprits, of course. A boss may have specific plans for a protégé, a minister for a congregation, one friend for another. And those plans may or may not be God's best for the other person. When picturing a special future for others, we must remember whose future it is—and ask the Holy Spirit's guidance in steering those we love toward their own unique tomorrow!

Are you ever tempted to impose your desires on the people you love? How can we guard against this tendency?

Tomorrow the LORD will do wonders among you.
—JOSH. 3:5

Fortunately, many people realize the importance of providing their children, spouse, or friends with a picture of a special future. These people know how to use words of blessing to help mold, shape, and guide others into God's full potential for them. Are you one of these people?

As an exercise in making this element of the blessing an integral part of your life, picture a special future for yourself. First, pray that the Holy Spirit will help you perceive the special tomorrow He has in mind for you. Next, list five of your best qualities or characteristics. (If this is hard, ask some friends for suggestions.)

Meditate on your list. Then write a short paragraph, based on these qualities, that pictures a special future for you. Read it aloud to yourself and let the words soak in. Don't worry about whether you can "carry through." You are not setting goals or making predictions. You are learning a new skill while opening your spirit to receive God's blessing in a more meaningful way.

_____

Accept your blessing in thankfulness and trust. In one way or another, your future will include "great wonders" from the Lord.

> *And now abide faith, hope, love, these three; but*
> *the greatest of these is love.* —1 COR. 13:13

During the past month, we have explored the fourth vital element of the blessing: picturing a special future for those we love. This element adds the spark of hope to the message we communicate. But as the apostle Paul reminds us, hope is rooted in an even greater motivation: love.

Because others love us, we are given the blessing.

Because of the love in our hearts, we can pass the blessing on to others.

And because of God's encompassing and redemptive love, the whole process is possible. We can receive the blessing directly from Him even if we never received it from our parents. We can reach past our own pain to bless others. We can continue to grow in relationship with Him and others.

Pray that you will continue to grow in faith, hope, and love as you depend on God's promises for your future and in picturing a special future for the people you love.

Do not grow weary in doing good.
—2 THESS. 3:13

During the past few months, we have looked at the first four elements of the blessing: *meaningful touch, spoken words, expressing high value,* and *picturing a special future.* These elements are building blocks of the blessing. But the mortar holding them together is an *active commitment.*

In order to be blessed, children need adults who will actively commit to them. Children must be encouraged in the areas in which they are weak. They need to be praised for their strengths. When they hurt, they must feel loving arms around them and must be gently helped back to their feet. They need their potential to be brought out into the open and developed—even if it takes evenings and weekends. These actions and attitudes are vital in bestowing the blessing.

Active commitment is the fifth element of the blessing.

Whoever compels you to go one mile, go with him two.
—MATT. 5:41

Most children dread at least one subject in school. For me (Gary), it was math. Only one month into my senior year, I was sure I would flunk geometry. My teacher thought so, too. My only solace was that more than half the class was flunking with me.

But one Monday we had a new teacher (the regular teacher had been transferred). This new teacher said something that changed my life: "If anyone fails this class, I have failed." He said he would do whatever it took—including special tutoring and weekend sessions—to see that we all learned and enjoyed geometry to the best of our abilities. He remained faithful to this commitment. What a turn-around struck that class. What we had once dreaded, we now anticipated. At the end of the semester, we all passed! I even received my first A in math! We all jumped around, hugging each other. And it was all because one man committed himself to a struggling bunch of students. In so doing, I realized later, he provided us with the fifth element of the blessing.

Today's verse is not specifically about blessing, but the point applies. Active commitment means going the second mile to give the blessing to others.

If a brother or sister is naked and destitute of daily food, and one of you says to them, "Depart in peace, be warmed and filled," but you do not give them the things which are needed for the body, what does it profit?

—JAMES 2:15–16

As we have seen, words of blessing alone are not enough. They must be backed by someone's commitment to see the blessing come to pass. This principle is the heart of today's verse. It's much like a "Peanuts" cartoon which appeared years ago. The dog, Snoopy, sits out in the cold, staring at his empty bowl. Two children see him and feel sorry for him, so they walk over and say, "Be of good cheer, Snoopy!" Then, satisfied, they leave him to his cold and hunger—definitely not cheerful and definitely not blessed.

Words of blessing without active commitment are about as useful as the promises a crooked politician shouts on election eve. Children of all ages need the daily "food and clothing" of love and acceptance. But words are not enough. If we "talk the talk" but fail to support them with active commitment, we leave our children undernourished and ill-clothed emotionally.

Can you think of a time in your life when a lack of commitment turned a verbal blessing into empty words?

*The God who has fed me all my life long to this day . . .
bless the lads.*
                                                    —GEN. 48:15–16

The blessings found in Scripture are much more than empty words. And they illustrate several ways we can infuse the element of active commitment into the blessings we give our children, a spouse, or others.

One outstanding aspect of Old Testament blessings, for instance, was the practice of committing the "blessee" to the Lord. Isaac blessed Jacob with these words:

May God *give you of the dew of heaven,
of the fatness of the earth* (Gen. 27:28, emphasis added).

Years later, as we see in today's verse, Jacob blessed his sons and grandchildren by calling on "the *God* who has fed me all my life."

Calling on the name of the Lord is one way to strengthen the element of active commitment in a verbal blessing.

I am the God of your father Abraham; do not fear, for I am with you.
                                              —GEN. 26:24

One reason the Old Testament patriarchs called on the Lord to confirm their blessings was because they were confident of His commitment to them.

Isaac, for instance, was reassured of the Lord's commitment during a difficult time in his life. Living in the desert, he knew his most precious commodities were the wells he dug for fresh water. But twice, he had been driven from wells his father had dug. Finally, he dug a third well. That night, God appeared to him and assured Isaac of His faithful commitment by saying, "Do not fear, for I am with you." To Isaac, those words of love and commitment must have been like a cool drink of water on a hot summer day.

God later echoed His words of commitment to Jacob. While fleeing Esau's anger, Jacob spent the night in the desert. There, God avowed His love and commitment: "I am the Lord God of Abraham. . . . Behold, I am with you . . . will not leave you until I have done what I have spoken to you" (Gen. 28:13,15).

Do you find it easy or hard to feel God's loving commitment to you? What experiences and activities help you know "I am with you"?

The LORD who made heaven and earth
Bless you from Zion! —PS. 134:3

Isaac and Jacob were secure in their relationships with God. As a natural extension of that certainty, they asked the Lord to bless others through them.

We frequently see this in churches today. For instance, last week, in churches all across the country, pastors closed the worship service with the words, "May the Lord bless you and keep you." By calling on God Himself to confirm their blessings with His power and might, they did the very thing Isaac and Jacob did with their children. Many churches practice children's dedications. A pastor who lays his hands on a child in blessing provides a beautiful picture. It portrays the congregations' active commitment to that child's well-being and their desire that God will bless this little one.

_____

In what ways do you think calling on the Lord to confirm a blessing strengthens the element of active commitment?

The everlasting God, the LORD . . .
neither faints nor is weary.
His understanding is unsearchable.
—ISA. 40:28

Why is it so helpful to invoke the Lord's name when giving the blessing? First, when we say, "May the Lord bless you," we recognize and acknowledge that any strength we have to bestow the blessing comes from an all-powerful God. Even our very breath of life to speak words comes from Him. We all tend to be inconsistent and stumble occasionally while trying to bless our children. In contrast, God remains changeless in His ability to give us strength to love our spouse and children the way we should.

Another reason to commit others (especially children) to the Lord is because doing so teaches them that God is personally concerned with their welfare. Stressing the fact that the Lord is interested in their being blessed is like introducing them to someone who can be their best friend and a personal encourager to whom they can draw close throughout their lives.

Calling on the Lord as part of a blessing acknowledges who we are and teaches who God is. This basic realism is a solid foundation for active commitment.

> *The Lord is my shepherd;*
> *I shall not want.*
> —PS. 23:1

Karen and Nichole were still in grade school when their father died of a heart attack. These children no longer felt his arms comforting them nor heard his encouraging words of blessing. But they did know for certain that Papa was with the Lord and that Jesus would confirm their blessing. Why such certainty? Because a wise father and mother had continually reassured them of this. Their mother, Lisa, remembers,

> Before Ray died, he used to gather us before dinner. We would stand in a circle, holding hands. Then Ray would thank the Lord for our day and for the food and ending with these words: "Lord Jesus, thank You that You are Karen's, and Nichole's, and Lisa's, and my shepherd. Thank You that You will never leave us or forsake us. Amen." This past year without Ray has been rough. But it has helped so much to be able to remind the children that Jesus is still their shepherd.

Bringing the Lord into our words of blessing gives children a sense of security that we frail humans cannot convey. With Jesus as their shepherd, they truly "shall not want."

Even the youths shall faint and be weary, . . .
but those who wait on the LORD
shall renew their strength.

—ISA. 40:30–31

Children need the certainty and security that comes from our committing them to the Lord and their blessing. *Everyone* needs that kind of confidence.

This does not mean we are not participants in bestowing the blessing. Sometimes we must summon all our creativity and ingenuity—and depend on the Holy Spirit's guidance—to meaningfully bless someone. Still, when we bless someone in the Lord's name, we acknowledge that only by God's strength and might will we ever be able truly to bless others. With this in mind, consider calling on the Lord for a blessing in such common situations as:

Bedtime: "May the Lord watch over you through the night and keep you safe, and may you continue to grow in His grace."

Before an exam: "May the God who made you and gave you your intelligence now give you courage as you approach this test—and may you relax in the confidence that you are loved by God and by us."

Before a business trip: "May God watch over you and bring you home safely to us. And may the Lord bless and prosper as you let Him show you how to conduct your business to His glory."

When we call on the Lord, we participate in His blessings.

> *Train up a child in the way he should go,*
> *And when he is old he will not depart from it.*
> —PROV. 22:6

Another helpful way to translate this verse would be, "Train up a child according to his bent. . . ." Such a translation highlights the second way active commitment can confirm our blessing. We commit our lives to the best interest of the people we love by giving time, energy, and resources, but more importantly, by paying close attention to each person's needs.

Jacob did this when he gave a custom-tailored blessing to each of his twelve sons and two grandchildren— "He blessed each one according to his own blessing" (Gen. 49:28). We, too, show active commitment when we apply the elements of the blessing to the recipient's individual situation. One daughter, for instance, might need a dozen hugs and kisses at night before going to bed, while her sister does well with two. One son might feel secure hearing encouraging words only once, while his brother may need to hear "You can do it" over and over again.

Blessing someone requires our taking a personal interest in that individual's needs.

And let us consider one another in order to stir up love and good works.
— HEB. 10:24

The better we know children, spouse, or friends and their unique set of needs, the more powerful and appropriate the blessing we give them. But please pay close attention to this next statement: *Physical proximity does not equal personal knowledge.* We can spend years under the same roof with someone and still be intimate strangers—unaware of the other person's real desires, needs, goals, hopes, and fears.

Many people feel they "know" another person's interests and opinions because they were interested in that one's life in the past. But people change! Doctors tell us every cell in a human body wears out and is replaced by new cells within a few years. Thoughts, dreams, and desires change, too. If we want to truly bless someone, we must pay attention to the unique person he or she is *now.*

For a few moments, think about someone on your "blessings" list. Mentally rehearse (or list) some of the challenges and joys confronting that person this week. Then write a brief blessing that pertains specifically to those issues you have listed.

> *Reuben, you are my firstborn,*
> *my might and the beginning of my strength,*
> *the excellency of dignity and the excellency of power.*
> *Unstable as water, you shall not excel,*
> *because you went up to your father's bed;*
> *then you defiled it.*
> —GEN. 49:3–4

Blessing others means being willing to do what is best for them—even correcting them when they are wrong. These tactics may seem the opposite of blessing another person, but they actually strengthen the blessing by showing our willingness to help the loved one grow.

We see this when we look at the blessing Jacob gave to his oldest son, Reuben. At first glance, this blessing looks more like a curse. If we look closely, however, we can see Jacob balanced words of praise with words of correction. He praised his son's positive qualities— his might, strength, dignity, and power. But then he pointed out a lack of discipline. Reuben's unbridled passions had led him to the bed of one of his father's concubines. By speaking words of correction, Jacob showed a commitment to helping his son live to his fullest potential.

Discipline can be a powerful way to bless others by expressing active commitment to their growth and well-being.

*MY SON, DO NOT REGARD LIGHTLY THE DISCIPLINE OF
THE LORD . . . FOR THOSE WHOM THE LORD LOVES HE
DISCIPLINES.*
—HEB. 12:5–6 NASB

It should not surprise us that blessing and discipline
go hand in hand. If we genuinely love someone, we
will not allow that person to stray into sin or be hurt
without confrontation or correction. As today's verse
indicates, the Lord Himself is our model for such loving
discipline.

By correcting us instead of merely ignoring our
wrong behavior, God treats us as His own children.
After all, how many people would discipline someone
else's child? But like a loving parent with a highly valued son or daughter, God cares deeply about our behavior. Our sons' and daughters' actions should also
concern us if we are going to truly bless them. We
should not shy away from loving discipline when it is
appropriate and in their best interest.

*We follow our Lord's example when we include loving discipline
along with our blessing.*

> *Now no chastening seems to be joyful for the present, but painful; nevertheless, afterward it yields the peaceable fruit of righteousness to those who have been trained by it.* —HEB. 12:11

Initially, disciplining someone can seem painful for both parties. Yet when you take that risk, you train that person and guide him or her to a place of peace and righteousness. Discipline is an important way of actively committing ourselves to a person's best interest.

All this is relatively easy to see when concerning children. But how does this concept apply to other adults? Are we in a position to discipline each other? It may be helpful to think in terms of *confrontation* rather than discipline when showing this form of active commitment to a spouse or friend. Our job is not to parent another adult, but we can confront harmful behavior and relational difficulties rather than sweeping these problems under the rug. If we truly care about that person and our relationship, we can do no less.

Do you need to confront someone in your life in order to give a blessing? How can you do so while respecting that person's right to make his or her own choices?

Apply your heart to understanding.
—PROV. 2:2

We have already looked at two ways in which we can demonstrate an active commitment in blessing others. First, we can commit them to the Lord. Second, we can seek their best interest.

We can also demonstrate an active commitment by becoming a student of those we wish to bless.

Becoming a student means setting aside enough time and energy to become involved in the other person's life—applying our hearts to understand that person. (The Proverb is about wisdom in general, but it certainly applies to understanding other people as well!) To study someone means listening to them express needs and concerns. This may mean doing some homework, becoming familiar with that one's work and hobbies.

This doesn't mean our interests and activities must be identical to those of the person we want to bless. But we cannot bless others until we pay close attention to their ideas, pains, hopes, and dreams.

What specific actions could help you become a student of your children, spouse, or friends? What barriers of time, insecurity, or interest hinder you?

> *Enlarge the place of your tent*
> *and let them stretch out the curtains of your*
> *dwellings; . . .*
> *for you shall expand to the right and to the left.*
> —ISA. 54:2–3

In my (John's) mother's modest Arizona condo stands a nondescript bookcase filled with seemingly unrelated publications. One shelf is crammed with theology and psychology books. Medical journals and genetics texts line another shelf. The third groans with past issues of *Heavy Equipment Digest* and "how to" books on operating bulldozers and earth movers.

Now, all this might indicate eccentric reading tastes unless you realize my mother has three sons. I am a Christian counselor and writer. My twin brother, Jeff, is a medical doctor specializing in genetic research and cancer. Our older brother, Joe, is an administrator who used to drive heavy equipment. My mother's odd assortment of reading material is actually a beautiful picture of her willingness to stretch herself "to the right and to the left" to study each son, including his interests.

Becoming an active student of those you bless may mean stretching your mind and heart to understand their interests.

I applied my heart to know,
to search and seek out wisdom and the reason of things.
—ECCL. 7:25

One important way to study your children, spouse, or others is to lovingly pursue communication. I (Gary) learned this lesson from my oldest son, Greg, when we were on a television talk show. The show's host asked Greg what parents could do to communicate with their children. Without hesitation Greg said, "Don't believe it when your son or daughter tells you they 'don't want to talk.' Sometimes I'll say that to Dad and Mom, but I don't mean it. I'm really hoping they will be persistent and help me talk about it."

We often encounter resistance when we try to understand others better, especially if our relationships have been strained, if we haven't been close to them before, or if they are uncomfortable or embarrassed to talk about themselves. When that happens, don't quit! Don't badger them or try to pry words out of their mouths. But apply your heart to learn the "reason of things" that pertain to them.

Pray that God will give you perseverance and sensitivity to be a student of others even when they resist communication.

For where two or three are gathered together in My name, I am there in the midst of them.

—MATT. 18:20

Sharing activities can help us become a student of those we wish to bless. This will draw us closer together and offer tremendous learning opportunities.

My (Gary's) younger son, Mike, and I went hunting together a few years ago. With book deadlines and a busy travel schedule looming, I was not eager to take a week walking up and down steep mountains. However, I felt this would be a tremendous opportunity to spend time with my son.

I was right. Sitting together on the flight, tramping through the woods, resting by the campfire—these provided unguarded moments for meaningful conversation. Without having to "manufacture" conversation, we talked about some of his dreams, his girlfriend situation, and more. In some ways, I felt reintroduced to my son.

You don't need to go hunting to share activities, of course. Camping, walking, doing needlework, putting photos in albums, studying the Bible, working puzzles, or just sitting outside in the twilight can produce the same results—if you remember to listen!

What activities do you and your family enjoy together? Which pursuits offer relaxed time for communication?

I will ask you something. Hide nothing from me.
—JER. 38:14

Asking questions can be yet another way to study our children. You may say, "But I don't know what to ask or how to get started!" Here are several questions you can ask in unguarded times at the hamburger place, at the ball game, or while taking a walk:

1. What do you daydream about most often?
2. When you think about being grown up, what would you enjoy doing?
3. Of all the people you have studied in the Bible, who would you want to be like? Why?
4. What do you believe God wants you to do for humankind?
5. What type of boyfriend or girlfriend is most attractive to you? Why?
6. What is the best part of your school day? What is the worst?

These are just starting points, of course. We can and should ask our children many more questions to help us learn about them. This will help us value them for who they really are.

_____

Taking the initiative to ask questions can be yet another way to become a student of our children.

I told you already, and you did not listen. Why do you want to hear it again? —JOHN 9:27

Have you ever carried on an entire conversation with someone while you were absorbed in the paper or the evening news? Most of us have—and the other person's frustration probably echoed that of the formerly blind man in today's verse. "Uh, huh" and "That sounds good, honey" accompanied by a rustle or commercial certainly does not communicate acceptance nor help us become a student of what the other person wants to share. We bless the important people in our lives by being emotionally present when they talk to us.

Giving our full attention to someone is far from easy. Conflicting distractions may demand our attention. We may be overwhelmed and just want to retreat. Unacknowledged anger may cause us to withdraw. And sometimes plain old selfishness keeps us from listening to others.

Becoming aware of our inattention is the first step toward changing it. Even setting aside fifteen minutes each day to pay full attention to someone we love can pay enormous blessing dividends.

What kind of circumstances tend to make you withdraw your attention from those you love?

Bright eyes gladden the heart.
—PROV. 15:30 NASB

One way to remind ourselves to listen actively is found in today's verse. Most of us have, at one time or another, walked into a room and seen someone's eyes "light up" when he or she sees us. The sparkle in another person's eyes tells us that person is interested in us and paying attention to our words.

An interesting study was conducted, based on this very verse. Several college men received pictures of ten women who were equally attractive. Each student was asked to rate the pictures from "most attractive" to "least attractive." These young men did not know that five of the women were given an eye-drop solution just before their pictures were taken. This solution dilated their pupils—which happens naturally when we are glad to see someone and are interested in him or her. The results of the study were predictable. The girls with "bright eyes" were chosen hands down as the five most attractive women.

Do your eyes "light up" when you listen to those you wish to bless? Your children or spouse will notice if they do or don't.

Create in me a clean heart, O God,
And renew a steadfast spirit within me.
—PS. 51:10

It is not always easy to bless others by giving them your full attention, but some practical steps can help you.

The simplest strategy (though not the easiest) is to turn off the TV, close the magazine, fold the paper. In other words, put distractions out of sight. Go to another room. Shut the door. If household bustle and chores threaten to divert your attention, take a walk or go to a restaurant.

Longer-range strategy may also be necessary. If you cannot give your full attention because you feel overworked or overwhelmed, plan ahead for "quality time" or even fundamental changes in your life-style. Schedule a "wind down" time after work to help you put the job on the back burner and be fully present at home. Reduce time pressure by weeding out your activities. Consciously set aside specific times to focus on your loved ones. No matter what measures you must take, the benefits make any sacrifices worthwhile.

_____

How can you be more "present" to the ones you love when you spend time together?

*Now may the Lord direct your hearts into the love
of God and into the patience of Christ.*

—2 THESS. 3:5

How do these everyday blessings demonstrate the crucial element of active commitment?

1. When I was thirteen, my dad trusted me enough to let me use his favorite hunting rifle when a friend and his father invited me to go hunting.
2. We had "family meetings" every two weeks. We were each encouraged to share goals and problems.
3. If it was really cold, my mom would get up early and drive me on my paper route.
4. When I had my appendix out, my parents were with me before and after the operation.
5. Sometimes I would come home from school to find a plate of cookies on the counter accompanied by a note from my mother simply saying she loved me.
6. My parents used to take me and my friend out for a special dinner sometimes.

In the long run, the only way to succeed in blessing others is to focus on God's incredible love for you and for the people you want to bless. This week, be conscious of leaning on that love and claiming Christ's patience as you pursue the business of blessing.

> *For He is the living God, and steadfast forever; His*
> *kingdom is the one which shall not be destroyed,*
> *and His dominion shall endure to the end.*
> —DAN. 6:26

Humans are incredibly complex. Today, if you would start listing all the wishes, opinions, goals, and dreams of the person you want to bless, it would take you a lifetime to complete the list. That is just the right amount of time needed to finish the course entitled, "Becoming a Student of Your Loved Ones." This is a class in which you will enroll if you are serious about bestowing an appropriate blessing on each person in your life.

Sound like a challenging course? It's one of the hardest you'll ever take. In fact, you probably won't be able to manage it on your own. Few of us can sustain unselfish love, especially on a long-term basis!

How do you muster the love, forgiveness, and stamina to be a student of others over the long term—even when their needs conflict with yours? You can only do this if you depend on the One who has been committed to you since before you were born and will still be devoted to you long after your death.

Lord, I want to give a blessing to those I love, but I know I don't have the stamina. Sustain me in Your spirit and bless me, so that in blessing others I am merely passing along Your love.

*Love . . . bears all things, believes all things, hopes
all things, endures all things.* —1 COR. 13:4,7

Many of us have shelves filled with notebooks from
marriage or parenting seminars. We have files of notes
from sermons. Typically, when we get excited about a
principle we read or a tape we hear, it can dramatically affect our lives. After a few weeks, however, that
book or tape usually ends up on a dusty shelf with
other inspirational materials.

As we have taught people about blessing their children, we have seen lives change drastically. For the
first time, many people have come to grips with
whether they ever received the blessing and are gaug-
ing how well they are doing in providing it for their
children. We hope you have already begun to see your
parents' home and your own in a new light. Yet like
any other call to commitment, the inner voice encouraging us to bless our children may grow faint as time
passes. That is why *perseverance* is a vital part of our
commitment to giving the blessing.

---

*Active commitment develops a stubborn streak. It perseveres even
when the novelty of giving a blessing wears off.*

> *But God, who is rich in mercy, because of His great*
> *love with which He loved us, even when we were*
> *dead in trespasses, made us alive together with*
> *Christ.*
> —EPH. 2:4–5

At one point in the classic musical, *Fiddler on the Roof*, Reb Tevye's oldest daughter tells him she wants to marry and then blurts out, "Papa, we are not asking for your permission; but we would like your blessing." That's an important distinction to remember when giving the blessing: it is not the same thing as giving permission or sanctioning behavior. As writer Lee Ezell points out about children:

> We . . . must find a way to bless them in spite of their behavior, just as our heavenly Father blesses us in spite of ours. . . . We don't have to agree with or be proud of our sons and daughters to love them. Although God is not always a proud dad, somehow His love continues to flow. . . . And God loved us way before we were lovable commodities! He didn't just decide to love us when we got humble; He didn't wait until we were begging for forgiveness either. But when we were "dead in trespasses and sins," He was extending His hand to us. Now He is speaking to us troubled parents when He tells us to [do the same].*

Search for ways to bless the ones you love regardless of how they behave.

*Lee Ezell, *Pills for Parents in Pain* (Dallas: Word, 1992), ch. 10.

Therefore if the Son makes you free, you shall be free indeed.
—JOHN 8:36

*C*ommitment is a frightening word to many people. To them, it signifies a loss of freedom, which really frightens people these days. Couples avoid marriage because they don't want to be "tied down." Students put off declaring a major from fear of cutting their options. Apartment dwellers even hesitate before signing a short-term lease.

Commitment doesn't have to signal the loss of freedom. In fact, true freedom is only found in the context of commitment. Without it, in the words of an old song, freedom becomes "just another word for nothing left to lose."

When you sign the lease, you're free to settle in and get comfortable. After you choose a major, you're free to dig into a satisfying course of study. When you marry, you're free to love freely and plan confidently. And when you commit your life to Christ, you become "free indeed."

Today we celebrate our forebears' commitment to the cause of freedom. This is a good day to celebrate the blessings that come with true commitment.

> *All of you be submissive to one another, and be*
> *clothed with humility.*
> —1 PETER 5:5

How can we establish a pattern of commitment that lets each element of blessing reside in our homes? The best way we know is found in a single word: *accountability*. Left on our own, most of us will forget or side-step some of the elements, but faithful friends can challenge us to stay on the path. Imagine someone asking what you did in providing meaningful touch or encouraging words for your spouse or children that week. Imagine someone inquiring how high your commitment to bless your family rated this week. Imagine having a place where you can admit your struggles and learn from other people's insights (and mistakes). This can happen during Sunday school at your church or in your home on a weeknight. The only requirements are the courage to ask honest questions, a loving spirit to share God's truth and your own insights—and the nerve to call one or more friends to join you in a covenant of accountability.

Blessings thrive within a context of accountability. Faithful friends can help us face problems and grow. Their love and emotional support can share our sorrow and double our joy.

And above all things have fervent love for one another, for "love will cover a multitude of sins."
—1 PETER 4:8

Accountability can also involve asking those you want to bless to hold you accountable. You can ask your spouse or a close friend how well you are doing in being a blessing to them. If your children are old enough, you can even ask them. Children will usually be honest, and you can learn valuable lessons from them—if you will take the time to listen.

Asking questions, and answering them, can be threatening. Even so, individual conversations offer tremendous evaluation. The feedback we receive from someone we want to bless can give us incentive to work on an area with which we struggle. And the act of asking is another way of expressing our faithful, continuing commitment.

———

Accountability to those we want to bless can train us to be even better vessels of blessing to them.

> *Many daughters have done well,*
> *But you excel them all.*
> —PROV. 31:29.

Commitment is costly. If you seriously want to bless those you love, expect to pay a price, especially in terms of time, energy, and effort.

Is the price worth it? Proverbs certainly seems to say it is. Proverbs 31 describes a woman who blesses her family in many ways. She is industrious and loving, has a positive outlook, and is committed to her husband and children. Her words to her family overflow with wisdom and kindness. And each of these admirable qualities was developed at the price of many early risings and many hours of hard work. She invested her energy in blessing her family—the same kind of energy that gets parents out of bed on the weekend to take their children camping or pushes husbands or wives to stay up late helping their mate complete a project.

Was it really worth all that effort? It was for this woman. Read what her family has to say about her and her decision to make a genuine commitment to them: "Her children rise up and call her blessed; / Her husband also, and he praises her" (v. 28).

If asked, would your family say that you have paid the price to bless them? If not, what obstacles stand in your way?

> *Therefore, my beloved brethren, be steadfast,*
> *immovable,always abounding in the work of the*
> *Lord, knowing that your labor is not in vain in the*
> *Lord.*
> —1 COR. 15:58

To provide the blessing to another person takes hard work, wrapped in the words "active commitment." It requires time to meaningfully touch and hug our children after school or before they go to bed. We need courage to verbalize words of love for our spouse. Wisdom and boldness are necessary to "bow our knees" to highly value those we love. And creativity is certainly a must to picture a future filled with hope and God's best for our loved ones' lives. But all this effort is worthwhile. One day, perhaps years later; that blessing will return. Your children will rise up and bless you. Even better, you'll experience the joy of seeing another person's life bloom and grow because you have been committed. This is a blessing in itself.

Blessing another person can be its own reward.

> *Cast your bread upon the waters,*
> *for you will find it after many days.*
> —ECCL. 11:1

Bubs" Roussel was only seventeen when World War II broke out and he joined the Army Air Corps. His assignment: a radio operator on a B-29 bomber making runs on Japan. The work was dangerous. And on December 13, 1944, Bubs's craft was one of four that did not return from a bombing raid. Along with the official notification of Bub's death, his parents received a letter that showed all their efforts to bless him had paid off:

Dear Folks:
    I have left this with instructions to send it on to you if anything happens to me. I send you my love and blessings. My life has been a full one. I have been loved like very few persons ever. I love you all with the best that is in me. It hasn't been hard for me, knowing you believe in me, trust me, and stand behind me in fair or foul. Knowing this has made me strong.*

Giving our children the blessing can be like casting bread upon the waters. In years to come, your blessings may return to you.

*Dewey Roussel, "Message of the White Dove," *Reader's Digest,* September 1985, p. 29.

Behold, now is the accepted time.
—2 COR. 6:2

Talking or reading about the blessing is good, but to put it into practice is even better. You can do this by planning an "evening of blessing" for the children in your life. Whether this evening comes once or several times a year, each child should experience the elements of the blessing in a special setting and a unique way. (We know several people who have coordinated their time of blessing with a birthday celebration.)

What happens during an evening of blessing? The details are up to you. We suggest you gather for a meal, then enjoy activities that celebrate the "guest of honor" and express how special he or she is. Next, take time for a prayer and a formal blessing, committing the child to the Lord. Continue the evening with a family activity, a talk session, or whatever would mean the most to your child. However you design this evening, it can be a meaningful time for you and your children.

Whether or not you have already practiced the blessing, consider whether "now is the accepted time" to plan an evening of blessing for someone you love.

> *That I may come to you with joy by the will of God,*
> *and may be refreshed together with you.*
> —ROM. 15:32

Children love surprises—but most children love anticipation even more. Therefore, if you plan a time of blessing for a child, let him or her know ahead of time. How much ahead will depend on the age of the child, but almost any child will love looking forward to a special event focused on him!

Ask the child ahead of time what he or she would like to have for dinner. Be prepared for peanut butter and hot dogs as a main course, topped off with chocolate cake for dessert (and Rolaids® on the side). This is not a time for correct nutrition, but an opportunity to honor someone. You may sneak in a vegetable or two. But most important is that your child can look forward to an evening fit for a "king" or "queen."

Plan to enrich your evening of blessing with anticipation and celebration—from the child's point of view

*Celebrate . . . with gladness, both with
thanksgivings and singing.*
—NEH. 12:27

Need some ideas for activities to use in "celebrating with gladness" a special evening of blessing (or any other time)? Try these:

1. Put together a slide show or picture album showing each year of the child's life. Or make a video of family members reminiscing.
2. List five to ten things you have appreciated about that child during the past year. (Choose character traits as well as accomplishments.) Say a word about how these character traits will help the son or daughter be a godly, helpful, or loving person in years to come.
3. Pick an everyday object and use it as a word picture to praise your child or to point out a talent God could use in the future.
4. Give your child a homemade gift. One mother gave her daughter a beautiful afghan she had spent months crocheting. This became the beginning of her daughter's hope chest.

Use your prayer time this morning to list ideas like these for expressing your love and appreciation. Ask for God's guidance in choosing the most effective possibilities for celebration.

> *By You I have been upheld from birth; You are He*
> *who took me out of my mother's womb. My praise*
> *shall be continually of You.*
> —PS. 71:6

One of the most powerful "blessing activities" you can give a child during an evening of blessing (or another special time, such as a birthday or Christmas) is to write out a "story of your birth" and read it aloud. Tell about the special events of the nine months before birth, the mad dash to the hospital, and the indescribable joy of seeing that child for the first time. Knowing they were planned and looked forward to blesses children immensely (regardless of whether they came in our timing or not).

If a child was adopted, write a story describing the hard work of applying for adoption, the difficulty of waiting, the thrill of getting the news. Stress how much the child was wanted and, if possible, point out how much love the birth mother showed in giving the child up for adoption.

You can find many creative variations of this blessing. One doting grandfather celebrated his first granddaughter's December 23 arrival with a sonnet about Advent and birth!

Use your imagination to spell out the message: "You're loved!"
"You're wanted!" "We're glad you're here."

Consecrate yourselves therefore, and be holy.
—LEV. 20:7 NIV

When the moment of formal blessing comes during your evening of blessing (or other occasion), take advantage of the solemnness of the moment. Sing a hymn or a familiar chorus to make a transition from fun activities. Or, light candles and gather in a circle. If your denomination allows, sharing Communion with older children is especially meaningful. This can also be a time to ask forgiveness if we have offended anyone in the family and a chance to focus together on the cup of blessing that represents Christ's love for us.

Then comes the time of blessing. Prepare a few short sentences ahead of time to read or recite. As you speak, lay your hand on the child's shoulder or head and look directly into his or her eyes. This can be moving, so don't be afraid of tears! The moment of formal blessing should be a holy time for the whole family.

Does the idea of giving a formal blessing make you feel uncomfortable? Give these feelings to the Lord and ask for courage to carry out the blessing anyway—for your sake and your child's.

> *And he blessed him and said . . .*
> —GEN. 14:19

Here is a sample of a formal blessing, given to a boy named Joseph, during a special evening of blessing:

> Thank You, Lord, for our son, Joseph. We ask You to be the Source of his joy and the Source of his life. Help us as parents to love Joseph as You would have us love him. Thank You for the way he is already growing into the unique person You designed him to be. Lord, we know how special Joseph is to You, and tonight may he realize how valuable he is to us now and forever. May he become all You want him to be and always know we are honored to be his parents. Bless us all now, for it's in Jesus' name we pray.

Use your quiet time today to write a formal blessing based on this model or your own words. Remember to attach high value, picture a special future, and express commitment.

*He who . . . is not a forgetful hearer but a doer of
the work, this one will be blessed in what he does.*
—JAMES 1:25

How are you doing at the everyday task of providing
a blessing? Let's look at the everyday blessings others
reported their parents gave them:

1. When my teacher didn't like me, my parents
   stood up for me.
2. My mother got interested in computers just because I was interested in them.
3. They could have just shipped my stuff, but my
   parents drove a U-Haul® trailer more than 1,800
   miles when I went off to college.
4. Dad gave up smoking because he knew how
   much it bothered Mom and us kids.
5. My father taught me how to budget my money.
6. Even though I didn't like it at the time, the
   chores my parents made me do helped me
   learn responsibility.
7. My parents always made sure I knew why I
   was being disciplined.
8. My father let me go with him on some business
   trips.
9. I realize now how hard my mother worked to
   take care of us all.

Don't forget to bless your family and friends every day!

> . . . *visiting the iniquity of the fathers upon the*
> *children to the third and fourth generations.*
> —EX. 20:5

We have been moving toward a deeper understanding of the difference the blessing can make for all people, especially children. Living for years in a "family of origin" leaves a profound mark on a child—in most cases, a positive one. Yet some homes leave an ugly mark of relational pain that their children, like Cain, must wear all their lives and may pass on to *their* children. This is where the terrible truth found in Exodus 20:5 rings clear: "the iniquity of the fathers" is passed through the generations.

As you have tried to weave the practice of blessing others into your life, you may have become painfully aware of a "blessing deficiency"—your own or someone else's—that limits your ability to bless others. If so, take heart. The generational cycle of missed blessings *can* be broken; we will see how in coming months. First, however, we will explore what happens when families withhold the blessing from their children.

_____

Approach the next few months with an attitude of prayerful expectancy. Ask God to make you aware of ways in which missed blessings may affect your current relationships.

You have not given the weary water to drink, and
you have withheld bread from the hungry.
—JOB 22:7

Not everyone who missed the blessing is consciously aware of this struggle in life. But people around them see it. An underlying sense of insecurity, an angry spirit, or a distant reserve can all be clear signs that a person's home did not provide the blessing.

What kinds of homes are these? Often, the parents simply lack the knowledge or skill to pass on the blessing. Other parents struggle with serious emotional or relational problems that can leave deep scars on their children. For whatever reason, these parents have withheld from their hungry children the blessing that could have sustained them in adulthood.

While counseling people throughout the country, we have observed many homes in which a "blessing deficiency" has scarred one or more inhabitants. And we have seen five general relationship patterns surface repeatedly in these homes. Over the next few weeks, we'll look at these patterns and how growing up with them can affect a person's ability to give the blessing.

Pray that God will bring healing in the blessing-deficient areas of your life and in the lives of people around you. Ask Him to show you how you can be actively involved in this healing.

> *Be kind to one another, tenderhearted, forgiving*
> *one another, even as God in Christ forgave you.*
> —EPH. 4:32

Before we tour the kinds of homes that withhold the blessing, we want to express a concern. We don't want these explorations to become ammunition to dishonor a parent. Nor do we want to offer an excuse on which to blame all present problems. Our aim is to inspire compassion, not to heap criticism on horrible parents. We want to make it possible for you to honor your parents (perhaps for the first time) and take your own responsibility for your behavior today.

Most parents truly love their children (even if they do not know how to show it) and have tried their best with the information they had. Even when this isn't true, the children of these parents cannot overcome their legacy of pain until they have learned to value their parents anyway and show forgiveness—just as God, in Christ, has forgiven them.

Are you aware of an undercurrent of blame in your own life or in the life of someone close to you? If so, pray for a heart of forgiveness. Or, at least pray for the grace to want to forgive. (God will take it from there.)

*Stand fast therefore in the liberty by which Christ
has made us free, and do not be entangled again
with a yoke of bondage.*
—GAL. 5:1

Finding freedom is one of our goals in examining the
ways families can withhold the blessing. Only when
you can truthfully look at your parents and your past
are you ever truly free to "leave" them in a healthy
sense and "cleave" to others in present relationships
(Gen. 2:24 NASB). If you carry anger or resentment
from the past, you are not free to "leave." Instead, you
are chained to the past and will probably repeat it.

Even if your family was a relatively healthy one that
blessed you profoundly, chances are that you are still
"blessing deficient" in certain areas. No parents are
perfect, and no parents can totally protect their children from hurt. You must come to terms with your
blessings deficits, no matter how minor. This will free
you to pass on a richer blessing to those you love. It
will also increase your compassion for those who
missed the blessing altogether.

*God's Word gives help and hope to deal with the lack of the family
blessing. But only when you face the truth about your past pain will
you be free to experience blessings for yourself and those you love.*

> *And they shall repair . . .*
> *the desolations of many generations.*
> —ISA. 61:4

You're just like your mother!"

"That's just the kind of thing your father would say!"

Such words are usually spoken in anger or jest, but they point to a bedrock reality: we learn our ways of relating to the world directly from the people who raised us. And they learned the same things from the people who raised them. This generational reality is the reason the "desolation" of missed blessing is carried over the years. But if we let it, the same reality can help us look at our upbringing with understanding instead of blame.

You may have grown up in a chaotic household where people solved problems by yelling and throwing things. Or your home may have been silent and cold, seething with repressed anger. But where did your mom or dad learn to yell or cover up anger at all costs? Your parents were greatly influenced by *their* parents and that experience reflects on you.

As you consider the type of home in which your parents grew, you may find answers to difficult questions about them. More important, you may learn to "repair the desolation of generations" by taking a new path.

I will not leave you orphans; I will come to you.
—JOHN 14:18

If you grew up in a blessing-deficient home, or are struggling to live with someone who did, you may find the next few weeks of meditation to be difficult. Even if you did grow up feeling blessed, you may discover some areas in your life in which you missed a blessing or failed to give one.

Before we explore the homes where blessings run short, therefore, stock up on blessing from your heavenly Father. Remember you belong to a God whose blessings are everlasting. From the very beginning of His relationship with us, He has promised abundant blessings—and He never reneges on His promises. Later, we will explore practical ways to claim His promises of blessing (even when we missed our family's blessing) and to generously pass His blessings to others. Meanwhile, hold fast to His promise of comfort. Even emotional orphans will receive the comfort of His eternal presence and substantial hope.

The beautiful King James translation of this verse is "I will not leave you comfortless." Draw hope from Christ's promise of comfort as you explore situations that may cause pain.

> *One part was rained upon, And where it did not*
> *rain the part withered.*
> —AMOS 4:7

In the springtime, the Seattle area is lush and green, drenched daily with refreshing showers rolling in from the sea. Just a few hours east, however, across the coastal mountain range, the land is semi-arid.

A similar phenomenon occurs in many homes. One child may be drenched with showers of parental blessings. But just "east" of that child at the dinner table may sit one or more siblings whose emotional lives are like parched ground. So few drops of blessing have fallen on the soil of their lives that emotional cracks have begun to form.

This was the case for Joyce and her older brother Jim. Joyce had been conceived to bolster a shaky marriage, but soon the father turned all his attention on Joyce as an escape from his marital problems. She became his confidante and companion, while he ignored his wife and son. The result was a lifelong legacy of pain for both children.

The first type of blessing-deficient home is the flood-or-drought home that blesses one child and withholds blessing from another.

*Now Israel loved Joseph more than all his children,
because he was the son of his old age. Also he
made him a tunic of many colors. But when his
brothers saw that their father loved him more than
all his brothers, they hated him and could not
speak peaceably to him.* —GEN. 37:3–4

We already know that Jacob, at the end of his life,
gave each son a special blessing. When his children
were young, however, Jacob only showered Joseph
with the blessing. It took that family at least a lifetime
to resolve the emotional havoc wrought by that flood-
and-drought blessing.

The beautiful tunic Jacob gave his youngest son was
a token of special acceptance, but it stirred hatred in
eleven brothers. This anger over an unfair distribution
of blessing reached such proportions that Joseph's
brothers nearly killed him!

Anger, resentment, and insecurity typically torment
children growing up in homes where the blessing is so
close, yet so far away. Like a thirsty man who sees rain
falling at a distance, these children quickly enter discouragement and depression. They usually develop a
deep sense of inferiority and jealousy. All of these
emotions, over time, feed anger and resentment. This
disrupts relationships between children and parents,
as well as among the children.

The angers and inequities in a flood-or-drought home can tear a family apart.

> *I knew you in the wilderness, In the land of great drought.*
> —HOS. 13:5

The story of Jim, the brother who was denied the blessing his sister Joyce abundantly received, illustrates the plight of the "drought" victim in a flood-or-drought family.

As a child, Jim typically responded to the unfair situation with anger—"acting up" and breaking things. But these childish bids for attention only brought angry tirades from his father instead of the closeness he craved. Over time, Jim developed a nagging insecurity about whether he was truly valuable as a person and worthy to be loved. Surely his father could not be wrong, he reasoned. Tragically, Jim also began to equate his lack of blessing with being a boy. Sexual confusion piled atop the pain of rejection. His anger at his favored sister and passive mother grew into a dislike for all women. For seven years, Jim tried to fill his lack of the blessing in homosexual relationships, reaping pain and emotional destruction.

Not everyone who is denied the blessing in this fashion will be drawn into a destructive life-style. However, the pain of receiving nothing while a sibling receives everything is strong enough to wreak havoc in a child's life.

Do you know anyone who has grown up in a feast or famine home? How has this upbringing affected him or her?

Then they took him and cast him into a pit.
—GEN. 37:24

Children who miss the blessing in a flood-or-drought home are not the only ones who face problems. The children who receive the lion's share of the blessing can also find themselves "cast into a pit" of one kind or another. We have often seen this in our counseling offices. For example, outstanding athletes often grow up feeling guilty about receiving the blessing in their family. Often, because of their physical abilities, they receive more praise than any brother or sister. We talked to one athlete, for example, who desperately wanted a close relationship with his brothers. The excessive attention his parents showed him kept his brothers at arm's length and left him aching with loneliness and a sense of rejection.

"Drought victims" are not the only losers in drought-or-flood homes. The "flood victims" also suffer.

Who were cut down before their time, whose foundations were swept away by a flood?

—JOB 22:16

Joyce, you remember, received all the elements of the blessing while her brother, Jim, received no blessing. But Joyce's blessing was actually a counterfeit; her father blessed her to meet his own needs, not hers. Over time, she became so dependent on him that she became emotionally enslaved.

Joyce's real difficulties began when she began to date. Acting like a jealous rival, her father pointed out every flaw in the young men Joyce dated. And her father had lavished so much attention on her that boys her own age paled in comparison. Joyce had never learned to share or compromise, so all her relationships with men were "disappointing" and short-lived.

She married in her early thirties to a man her father chose. Not long afterwards, she was in the counselor's office complaining about her husband. The "things he expected"—such as paying attention to *his* needs— were beyond her comprehension or willingness to give.

Each child needs to be singled out sometimes for special praise or recognition. But if the elements of the blessing fall exclusively on one child, serious problems can develop for each child in the family.

*Every good gift and every perfect gift is from
above, and comes down from the Father of lights,
with whom there is no variation or shadow of
turning.*

—JAMES 1:17

Is it necessary to love everybody equally in order to
give a satisfactory blessing to the people in your life?
The answer is no—and it's a good thing, because loving everybody equally is humanly impossible! Very
few of us can honestly claim to love friends, co-
workers, fellow church members, or even children exactly the same way. You may feel especially drawn
to—or irritated by—someone who is much like you.
Your feeling about being male or female may influence
your relationships with members of the opposite sex.
You may experience a strong bond of protectiveness
for a vulnerable sibling, a threat from an assertive co-
worker, an unreasonable resentment toward a child
who reminds you of your mother.

Pretending that such natural bonds and clashes don't
exist won't help you bless others more fairly. Instead,
acknowledge your unequal feelings and confess them
to God (not the person in question!). Rely on what you
have learned about the blessing—and on the good gift
of God's perfect love—to "bless them anyway," no matter how you feel.

---

*You probably can't avoid unequal feelings about people, even your
own children. But you can give each person the blessing he or she
needs.*

> *Therefore I turned my heart and despaired of all the labor in which I had toiled under the sun.*
> —ECCL. 2:20

Tall, handsome, and athletic, Craig looked more like a "big man on campus" than a psychiatric patient—until you saw the thick bandages on his wrists. He was in the hospital because he had recently tried to take his life. What caused this young man so much pain that he could no longer face the future? In his home, the blessing was always just beyond his grasp—like the proverbial carrot dangling in front of a horse's nose.

Craig's father, a respected engineer, demanded excellence from himself and expected nothing less from his family. Because of his critical attitude and high expectations, his blessing had become like the mechanical rabbit at a dog race—running slowly enough to excite the chase, but too fast to be caught. Craig's accomplishments could never quite reach his father's standards, especially when it came to school. But Craig kept trying. What finally triggered his suicide attempt was the news that, for the first time in his three years at college, he would receive a *B*!

The home holding the blessing just out of reach sends its children on a perpetual and futile chase for a blessing they can never achieve.

Let me find favor in your eyes, and whatever you
say to me I will give.   —GEN. 34:11

Success" was somewhere on the cover of every book and magazine in Robin's home while she was growing up—and success was the unspoken condition for earning her parents' blessing. But success meant something different to each parent and trying to "find favor" in their eyes eventually put Robin in a terrible "double bind."

To please her father, a prominent businessman, Robin majored in marketing and landed a prestigious entry-level job, where she advanced quickly. He was immensely proud of her success. Then she married a junior executive and soon gave birth to two boys. And her mother (who had never worked outside the home) clearly expected Robin to do everything for her children that she had done. Before long, Robin found herself mercilessly pulled in two directions—keeping a killer pace at work to earn her father's praise and trying to be "supermom" to reach her mother's blessing. After several years of a killing schedule, the pressure became too much, and her emotional life shattered.

When both parents hold the blessing out of reach, their children can be pulled apart trying to please them.

*Then I looked on all the works that my hands had done
and on the labor in which I had toiled;
and indeed all was vanity and grasping for the wind.*
—ECCL. 2:11

The hurried pace of our culture makes it easy to be "driven" to the breaking point. Unfortunately, people who have missed the blessing are especially susceptible to this kind of frenzied activity. In reaching for parental acceptance, they easily become workaholics.

How does this happen? In their perpetual chase for the "carrot" dangling out of reach—their family's blessing—these men and woman work hard and often achieve substantial success in their chosen professions. Their efforts bring an abundance of praise and appreciation (not to mention money!). And this positive reinforcement keeps them moving, but does not satisfy their deep need for the missing blessing. So the accolades and material rewards and the satisfaction of achievement just keep these people driving forward, still trying, somehow, to reach the real blessing.

Does any area of striving in your life bring you satisfaction? Pray for insight to recognize any patterns of drivenness resulting from a missed blessing.

And what does the LORD require of you
but to do justly,
to love mercy,
and to walk humbly with your God?
—MIC. 6:8

How do you tell the difference between high standards and perfectionism? Between being driven and having high aspirations? Between motivating a child and holding the blessing just out of reach?

Remember the blessing itself is a high motivator, more potent than any set of impossible expectations could be. But more important, if you want to prevent the discouragement and drivenness accompanying the carrot-and-stick blessing, compare your expectations to God's. Today's verse lists the essentials from God's point of view. They aren't easy! But note that being sinless or mistake-proof is not on the list. God has no requirement for top grades or material success or marital status—and no condition for measuring up to other people's expectations. Instead, God's highest standards involve loving relationships with Him and other humans.

Do you dare ask more—or less—of yourself or others than the Father of the Universe asks?

> *Hear this, you who swallow up the needy....*
> *making the ephah small and the shekel large,*
> *falsifying the scales by deceit.*
> —AMOS 8:4–5

In some homes, the blessing is given to a child, but at a terrible price. Read the painful words of one woman who wrote to a national columnist:

> Ever since I was a little girl, my mother made me feel guilty if I did not do exactly as she wanted. Dozens of times she has said, "You will be sorry when I am in my coffin." I was never a bad girl. I always did everything she requested me to do.... Both my parents are eighty-two. One of these days my mother will die, and I am terrified of what it will do to me.*

In homes like this, a terrible transaction takes place—one as wicked as the unfair commerce in Israel condemned by the prophet Amos. A child is coaxed by guilt or fear into forfeiting all rights to his or her goals and desires. In return, the child gets a blessing that lasts only until the parent's selfish desire beckons.

In the third kind of home that withholds the blessing, a pitifully small blessing is given along with a significant burden.

*Quoted by Roger Hawley, "The Family Blessing: Implications for Counseling." Unpublished paper presented at the Texas Council of Family Relations Conference, 1983.

Every morning [the Lord] brings His justice to light;
He never fails,
but the unjust knows no shame. —ZEPH. 3:5

Nicole's parents divorced when she was nine years old. Six months later, after a whirlwind romance, her mother remarried. One evening, while Nicole's mother was away, her stepfather entered her room. In an evening of horror and shame, Nicole joined the ranks of sexual abuse victims. Then her stepfather proposed a vicious bargain: if Nicole ever mentioned what had happened, he would divorce her mother and leave them both to "starve on the street." But if she told no one, he would be nice to her and her mother.

Both of them kept their part of the bargain. Fear and shame kept Nicole quiet. And her stepfather went on with his life and marriage as though nothing had ever happened. He even treated her decently after that one event. But Nicole paid a terrible price for her silence. Over the years, unable to share her deepest hurt and pain, she remained isolated, held hostage by painful memories. Only years later, when she broke down and shared her secret with her loving husband, did she begin to find freedom from her unfair burden.

Any blessing extended with a burden attached is a counterfeit blessing with a painful legacy of shame.

But let each one examine his own work . . . For each one shall bear his own load. —GAL. 6:4–5

Not all "blessing bargains" are as ghastly as the two we have examined, of course—and not all are made by parents. Few of us are immune from letting our needs and expectations influence the way we bless others. These bargains are rarely spelled out verbally and are often unconscious:

"Sure, I'll bless you—if you spend most of your time with me."

"I'll bless you—if you don't embarrass me."

"I'll bless you—if you keep your weight down and don't let yourself go."

"I'll bless you—if you bless me."

All of these bargains use the blessing as a tool to get what we want from others. We use them to make our lives easier by making them carry some of our emotional load. Some may be more innocuous than others, but all are rooted in selfishness. And all have the same result: they give our blessing a hollow ring.

Lord, keep me aware of selfish motivations as I give the blessing to others. Remind me that depending on You to meet my needs and help me carry my own load is the best way to avoid putting unfair burdens on others.

*Fathers, do not provoke your children, lest they
become discouraged.*
—COL. 3:21

Jim was confused and brokenhearted. At nineteen, he
was ordered out of his parents' home by his father, and
he didn't know where to turn. What unpardonable sin
had he committed? Open rebellion? Lying? Stealing?
For Jim's father, it was something worse. Jim had decided not to follow in the footsteps of his father, grandfather, and great-grandfather and be a minister!

Sound incredible? This kind of separation happens
every day to sons or daughters who break a family tradition. We have seen it with a son who refused to take
over his father's garage, a daughter who dared vote
Republican, the son who married "the wrong kind of
girl," the daughter who turned down a bid to join her
mother's sorority. This separation occurs when parents
feel cheated out of something they expected from their
children. They withhold their blessing from that child
as punishment.

*The fourth home that withholds the blessing withdraws acceptance
as punishment for breaking unyielding family traditions.*

> *So I gave them over to their own stubborn heart,*
> *To walk in their own counsels.*   —PS. 81:12

Everyone in the family suffers when parents withhold the blessing to punish those who break tradition. Obviously, the child who is denied the blessing will experience ongoing pain. Siblings also suffer—even those who have conformed to family tradition. Such an unyielding attitude can force a brother to "choose sides" with his parents against another brother and force one sister to sneak out to visit another. Holidays and special family events can be ruined because of the iciness that forms the moment the "outcast" walks in the door.

Even parents who withhold the blessing under such circumstances suffer from the rupturing of a precious relationship piled atop their grief over a broken tradition. What a price to pay for the sake of being right!

When the blessing is used as a manipulative tool and a weapon of punishment, everyone suffers.

*If anyone does not obey our word in this epistle . . .
do not keep company with him, that he may be
ashamed. Yet do not count him as an enemy, but
admonish him as a brother.* —2 THESS. 3:14–15

Eddie and Belle's oldest son, Don, had a long-standing
drinking problem that was getting worse. Through his
struggles—embarrassment, job losses, even jail—Don's
parents had never withheld their blessing. Although
they never approved of his behavior, they prayed for
him, counseled and encouraged him, and bailed him
out numerous times. But when he began to physically
abuse his wife and children, they made a painful decision: no more financial support until their son attended
an alcoholic treatment program.

Eddie and Belle's tough love was *not* the same as
breaking an unyielding tradition. They loved him and
wanted the best for him as a person even more than
they loved their relationship with him. Therefore, they
were willing to confront him and even risk losing him.
Biblically and relationally they were on firm ground to
withhold that portion of their blessing from their son.

*Pray for the discernment to distinguish tough love, based on matu-
rity, integrity, and courage, from punishment, based on hurt pride
and unyielding expectations.*

Today, if you will hear His voice,
do not harden your hearts.
—HEB. 3:15

Parents who wave the banner "Unyielding Traditions Live Here" know the impact of their decision to withhold their blessing—and that is exactly why they do it. Their pride is hurt; now their children will also hurt.

As the years pass, the parents' position can harden. They are unwilling to give an inch, as if doing so meant giving a mile. They can sit through sermon after sermon about forgiveness, never misunderstanding the message, but hardening their hearts to the Spirit's promptings.

These homes operate by the unspoken rule: fulfill every expectation, and the blessing will be given. Travel a different road, and expect to wander far from the shelter of acceptance. This is the fourth home that commonly withholds the blessing, and it can leave both parent and child forever in an emotional winter.

Lord, whatever You want to teach me about forgiveness and reconciliation, teach me to hear Your voice. Show me how to live in the springtime of Your love, not the frozen winter of resentment.

*If anyone comes to Me and does not hate his father
and mother, wife and children, brothers and sisters,
yes, and his own life also, he cannot be My disciple.*
—LUKE 14:26

These words of Jesus, of course, need to be taken in
the context of the whole gospel and read with an understanding of biblical language. In Scripture, "love"
and "hate" are often contrasted to distinguish "good"
from "better." In telling us to hate our families, in other
words, Jesus was emphasizing we are to give God priority, even over our families.

Nevertheless, Jesus' strong language should hit us
full blast whenever we are tempted to withhold our
blessing as punishment for a loved one's going against
our wishes. In the long run, our children are responsible to God, not to us. The same is true for a spouse,
friends, or even our co-workers. We, too, are asked to
give God, not our wishes and desires, first place in our
lives.

When we make our blessing dependent on doing
what we want, what we think is right, or what we
think is important, we may manipulate the other person into disobeying God. This forces him or her to
choose between God . . . and us.

*Father, as I sort through complicated motives for blessing and not
blessing, help me remember those I love must answer first to You,
not to me.*

> *For they shall eat, but not have enough.*
> —HOS. 4:10

In this final type of home, a child does receive the blessing, but only a partial one. This happens most commonly when a parent is absent from the home and unable to consistently bless the child.

Many different circumstances can leave children feeling half-blessed. The death of a parent, for example, can leave a blessing-sized hole in a child's psyche that the surviving parent can never completely fill. The same may be true when one parent is prevented by physical or emotional barriers from being fully "present" to a child.

Especially painful are those situations in which—from the child's perspective, at least—the absent parent has a choice in the situation. In cases of divorce, abandonment, or adoption, the child asks not only "Why weren't you here to bless me?" but "Why did you choose to leave me?"

In the next few days we will explore some of the scenarios that can leave a child feeling still hungry for a blessing. Through the week, pray for the children and adults for whom choice or circumstances have resulted in blessings that are less than complete.

*For the LORD God of Israel says
that He hates divorce.*
—MAL. 2:16

Regardless of your feelings on whether divorce is permissible for Christians, it's easy to see that even a "friendly" divorce can damage the spirits of all involved, especially children. For example, one parent usually retains custody and the other moves out. Typically, the children are left with a partial blessing as the other parent moves out of their everyday lives.

This scenario is not inevitable. But studies have shown that during the first year after a divorce, noncustodial parents (usually fathers) see their children regularly and often shower the children with gifts and attention. After a year, however, the inconvenience of visitation begins to take its toll, and the contact between the noncustodial parent and the child usually decreases. After three years, many noncustodial parents see their children once a month or less—and the children are left with a growing blessing deficit.

The absence of one parent's consistent presence after a divorce leaves a blessing vacuum in a child's life. Surely that's one reason God says, "I hate divorce."

> *Why did you flee away secretly, and steal away*
> *from me, and not tell me.*
> —GEN. 31:27

Desertion by a parent can be harder on a child than losing that parent's blessing in any other way. When a parent dies, a child knows he has lost all opportunity to regain a missing part of the blessing from that parent. When parents divorce, the noncustodial parent is usually available at least part of the time. Deserted children know "out there somewhere" is a living person who still has the power to bless—but has chosen not to do so. This bitter knowledge leaves a legacy of questions and unresolved pain.

"Why did Mom (or Dad) go away?"

"What is wrong with me?"

"Men (or women) leave their families. How can I ever trust one?"

"When I grow up to be a man (or woman), will I do this terrible thing, too?"

Do you know someone who struggles with these questions? Only a cruel dealer deliberately passes out only half the cards a child needs to gain the blessing.

*For you . . . received the Spirit of adoption by
whom we cry out, "Abba, Father." The Spirit
Himself bears witness with our spirit that we are
children of God, and if children, then heirs.*
—ROM. 8:15–17

We commonly see another group of children in counseling who struggle with gaining only part of the blessing. These are adopted children who have received a full blessing from their adoptive parents, but still wonder, "Why did my natural parents leave me?"

Even when a child is totally secure in his adoptive parents' love, this question can arise. Sometimes it takes the form of misbehaving to see if the adoptive parents will "leave me like my natural parents did." Other children join clubs or pay organizations to find their natural parents, in an attempt to regain the part of the blessing they feel they lost.

All of this is understandable and, if handled right, can reaffirm their blessing. By providing the five elements of the blessing, backed by God's unchanging love, adoptive parents can give their children the security and self-confidence to face these questions. The children can search for the answers in a healthy way, without being dependent on their natural parents' blessing.

It helps to remember that, in Christ, we are all adopted children of a heavenly Father—but fully heirs to His blessing.

> *And the king said, "Divide the living child in two,*
> *and give half to one, and half to the other.*
> —1 KINGS 3:25

Any situation that results in a partial blessing—death, divorce, desertion, adoption, or even the emotional inability of one parent—leaves children naturally longing for the missed part of the blessing. This is true even when the parents who *do* bless the children are faithful in expressing love and acceptance.

Unfortunately, this natural tendency to seek the missing piece of the blessing can easily lead to envy, anger, and resentment. Adoptive parents may feel defensive when their adopted child seems obsessed with finding her birthparents. Parents who struggle to raise children alone may resent the child's interest in the other parent, who contributes little beyond an occasional birthday present. Unless parents are careful, their emotional tugging makes a child feel divided. Therefore, custodial parents must realize the child's desire for the missing part of their blessing does not negate the blessing they have received, but rather affirms it.

Custodial parents who allow their children freedom to seek the blessing of the absent parent give those children a tremendous gift of wholeness.

*And I thank Christ Jesus our Lord who has enabled
me, because He counted me faithful.*
—1 TIM. 1:12

My (John's) mother and father divorced when I was
thirteen months old. My mother retained custody of
my older brother, my twin brother, and me. As I have
read books on single parenting, I have found that my
mother could be on the cover of those books as a tremendous example. To this day, I cannot remember her
criticizing my father or building walls to keep us from
contacting him.

My mother is a very loving person. She made sure
that anger, discouragement, or weariness did not
cause her to neglect her own blessing. But my mother
is also very wise—wise enough not to question the ad-
equacy of her love when, after several years, my father wanted to re-establish contact with us. As a result,
my brothers and I enjoy a growing relationship with
my father, while remaining close to our mother. We
have these good relations in large part because Mom
did not curtail our natural desire to make contact with
our father.

*The blessing can thrive in less-than-ideal circumstances when it is
not used as a weapon or as a bargaining tool.*

The generous soul will be made rich,
And he who waters will also be watered himself.
—PROV. 11:25

In contrast to all the pictures of blessing-deficient homes, absorb these pictures of a home rich in blessing, which people have shared with us:

1. My parents were good examples of how a Christian marriage should function.
2. When I was discouraged about my boyfriend breaking up with me, my father took extra time just to listen to me and cry with me.
3. My parents never acted like they were perfect, and they never expected us to be perfect either.
4. Now that I'm an adult, I appreciate how my father taught me to communicate with him. That has helped me know how to talk to my husband.
5. My mother would let me explain my point of view on issues—even when she disagreed. She always made me feel my opinion was important.

Father, examining my blessing deficits can make me sensitive to blessing others more fully, but it can also make me selfish and introverted. Teach me to reach out even as I look inward.

He shall deliver you in six troubles,
yes, in seven.   —JOB 5:19

We have looked at five different homes that withhold the blessing from their children: (1) The "flood and drought" home, drenching one child and parching another; (2) The "stick and carrot" home which dangles the blessing forever just out of reach; (3) The "bad bargain" home, offering a small blessing with a large burden; (4) The "please me or else" home in which the blessing is dependent upon meeting parents' expectations; (5) The "missing piece" home in which the blessing is absent from at least one important person.

What kind of impact do these homes have in the lives of those who grow up in them? Each individual is unique, but in our counseling we have identified seven typical responses among those whose young lives were "blessing deficient." Knowing these characteristics may help you identify and understand someone who has grown up apart from the blessing (perhaps even yourself).

_____

As we explore the consequences of missed blessings, focus special attention to the daily Scriptures, which point to Christ's offer of delivery from each difficulty.

> *Yes, she will seek them, but not find them.*
> —HOS. 2:7

> *The Son of Man has come to seek and to save that*
> *which was lost.*
> —LUKE 19:10

We have examined several examples in which children have reacted to missing the blessing by beginning a lifelong search. Unfortunately, these "seekers" never know when they've found what they're looking for. Unsure of how acceptance feels—or should feel—they don't recognize it when they have it.

Seekers, therefore, are those who are always searching for intimacy, but can seldom tolerate it. For instance, they may love the excitement of courtship, but grow uncomfortable in the daily closeness of marriage. The lack of a blessing in their past leaves them uncomfortable in receiving it from a spouse—and they may become restless. Seekers can even struggle with accepting God's unchanging love for them because of the lack of permanence in the blessing in their early lives.

What "seeking" elements do you see in your life or in the life of a loved one? What does it mean to you to know that Christ is seeking you?

I am feeble and severely broken;
I groan because of the turmoil of my heart.
                                    —PS. 38:8

I will . . . bind up the broken and strengthen what
was sick.
                                    —EZEK. 34:16

When trying to assess environmental damage in a region, ecologists pay special attention to certain species of songbirds. Disruption in the nesting or mating habits of these delicate creatures can send an early warning of pollution that will eventually endanger humans.

In a way, the people we call "the shattered" are like the songbirds. These people's lives have been deeply troubled or destroyed by a corrupted home "habitat." They experience deep-seated anxiety, depression, and emotional withdrawal and may even be pushed to suicide. It's difficult to pinpoint why some people will go to pieces over a lost blessing while others live more or less normal—if restricted—lives. But these extreme cases point out the existence of the pain in all of us.

In a sense, the shattered are simply those who suffer more drastically from the pain that afflicts all those who have come from a blessing-deficient home. Christ offers healing both for them and for the "walking wounded."

> *And look—he eats,*
> *but . . . his soul is still empty.*
> —ISA. 29:8

> *He has filled the hungry with good things.*
> —LUKE 1:53

Like a two-thousand-pound sponge, people who are smotherers react to missing their parents' blessing by wanting more . . . more . . . more! These "needy" people tend to suck every bit of life and energy from a spouse, child, friend, or entire congregation. Their past has left them so emotionally empty that they smother others with their unmet needs or, like parasites, drain others of their desire to listen or help.

Unfortunately, smotherers usually make their problems far worse through their overwhelming neediness. When friends and family finally tire of carrying their emotional weight, smotherers feel rejected. Deeply hurt again, they never realize they have brought this pain on themselves. They may end up pushing away the blessing other people offer when actually, they desperately need it.

_____

How can you extend the blessing to a smotherer without being overwhelmed by his or her neediness?

Therefore their anger was greatly aroused . . . .and they returned home in great anger.
—2 CHRON. 25:10

*[The Lord] has sent Me . . .
to proclaim liberty to the captives.*
—ISA. 61:1

Today's verse refers to the resentment of Israelite troops who had been gathered, promised good pay, then fired. But their anger characterizes many people who have been wronged at home by being denied the blessing.

Some people go through their entire lives with a chip on their shoulder, daring other people to get close. Anger is always under the surface, showing up in their temperamental outbursts, vicious sarcasm, or—turned inward—depression and self-destructive behavior. Usually, the ultimate reason is because parents denied them their blessing in the first place.

As we have seen, anger chains people. Many adults are emotionally chained to their parents because they can neither forgive or forget that they were not blessed. As a result, the rattle and chafing of emotional chains distract them from intimacy in other relationships.

Do you know what it's like to live with an angry person—or live in the chains of ongoing anger? Pray for liberation and healing.

*Why do you commit this great evil against
yourselves, to cut off from you man and woman,
child and infant.*
—JER. 44:7

Draw near to God and He will draw near to you.
—JAMES 4:8

Once burned, twice shy" the old proverb states. This
could be the motto of some who have missed the blessing in childhood. After losing the blessing once from
an important person, they spend a lifetime protecting
themselves from its ever happening again. Consciously or unconsciously, with words or gestures, they
cut themselves off from spouse, children, and close
friends—keeping those who care about them at arm's
length.

Unfortunately, detachment works. Those who strive
to protect themselves this way usually succeed—at the
price of lifelong loneliness and often emotional at-
rophy.

In Scripture, the words "cut off" often refer to death
and desolation. Those who are detached from their
families and communities will wither and die, just as
a cut-off branch shrivels and browns. Those who
choose it voluntarily, as a form of protection, punish
themselves most.

---

*What are some of the tactics—and consequences—of emotional de-
tachment? Is this a problem for you or someone you love?*

It is vain for you to rise up early,
To sit up late,
To eat the bread of sorrows.
—PS. 127:2

Come to Me, all you who labor . . . and I will give
you rest.
—MATT. 11:28

In this category, line up extreme perfectionists, workaholics, notoriously picky house cleaners, and generally demanding people who try to get their blessing the old-fashioned way: by earning it. However, the blessing is a *gift;* it cannot be bought. You can find some counterfeit blessings for sale—at incredible prices—but they last only as long as the "showroom shine" on a new car. In real life, such counterfeit blessings rust and corrode once they leave the showroom floor.

Missing their parents' blessing pushes these people to rise up early and stay up late, tilting at a windmill named "accomplishment" in an illusory attempt to gain love and acceptance. If they continue their vain strivings, they end up burned out and disillusioned, still without their blessing.

Not every driven person is a recognizable workaholic. What other forms could this drive to earn the blessing take? How does Christ's promise of rest speak to your driven tendencies?

> *Why do you spend money for what is not bread,*
> *and your wages for what does not satisfy?*
> *Listen diligently to Me, and eat what is good,*
> *and let your soul delight itself in abundance.*
> —ISA. 55:2

Many people who have missed their parents' blessing look for that lost love in all the wrong places. As we mentioned earlier, unmet needs for love and acceptance can tempt a person toward sexual immorality— in an attempt to meet legitimate needs through illegitimate ways. This category also includes substance abusers. Too often, a drink or a pill is taken initially to try to cover the hurt from empty relationships past or present. Alcoholism or drug abuse can become a counterfeit way to try to gain the deep emotional warmth that comes with the blessing.

In a recent study of compulsive gamblers, more than 90 percent of the men studied were found to have "dismal childhoods, characterized by loneliness and rejection."* In other words, missing the elements of the blessing in a home can seduce a child into choosing immoral relationships, alcoholism, or even compulsive gambling as an attempt to fill missing relationship needs.

How do you extend a healthy blessing to someone who is accustomed to seeking it in unhealthy places?

*Richard A. McCormick, "Affective Disorders Among Pathological Gamblers Seeking Treatment," *American Journal of Psychiatry,* vol. 141, no. 2, p. 215.

You shall be a blessing.
Do not fear, let your hands be strong.
—ZECH. 8:13

After reading of all the damage a missed blessing can cause, do you feel a little gun-shy about relationships? Maybe you're freshly aware of ways you have failed the people you love. Or do you feel the pain of your own missed blessing so acutely that you fear passing it to someone else? Family history, mixed motives, expectations. What if you communicate the wrong message? What if you hurt when you want to help? What if . . .

Enough! This blessing business is important, but it's not all up to you! Yes, at times you have surely been less than a blessing to those you love. Chances are, it will happen again! Those are just the facts of sinful human nature. But you serve a God who is powerful enough to redeem sin, to make imperfect humans whole, to bless His people abundantly. Rest in Him. Trust Him. Give Him your fears. And then move on. "Let your hands be strong."

Lord, I become discouraged whenever I start feeling that blessing others is all up to me. In Your strength, however, I can be strong. Teach me to be a channel of Your blessing.

> *You have given him his heart's desire,*
> *and have not withheld the request of his lips.*
> —PS. 21:2

Missing the blessing in childhood can be painful and damaging, but it need not be fatal—or final. With help, even the "blessing deficient" can join the ranks of "the blessed." Rather than being locked into repeating the past, we can grow to become the people God wants us to be. So instead of looking down and losing hope, we should look up to the incredible provision of a blessing that can overflow in our lives. This blessing can replace a curse with contentment and make our lives a blessing for those around us.

Over the next few weeks, we will explore several ways you can recover from missing the blessing or reach out to someone else who has missed it. These recommendations are not a simple formula, nor do they guarantee an instant cure. However, we find that many who have applied these principles have received hope and healing.

Father, thank You for the magnificent gift of Your blessing, which You do not withhold from me. Teach me now to learn to accept it so I in turn may bless others.

And you shall know the truth, and the truth shall make you free.
                                        —JOHN 8:32

The road to blessing begins with a difficult first step: We must be honest with ourselves.

All of our counselees are required to memorize today's verse. The truth Jesus talks about in this verse refers to knowing Him in all His purity. Christ offers no cover-ups and no denials of problems. When we know the truth, we begin walking in the light that exposes darkness; and it alone can begin to set us free.

Many of us need to shine truth's searchlight on our past. Only then can we walk confidently into the future.

Being honest with your feelings about missing the blessing is the important first step toward healing and restoration.

> *If I say, "I will forget my complaint,*
> *I will put off my sad face and wear a smile,"*
> *I am afraid of all my sufferings.*
> —JOB 9:27–28

Many people who have missed the blessing try to explain, or avoid admitting, the obvious in their lives. They draw imaginary pictures of their past, or deny the real problems that exist. In this attempt to protect themselves or their parents, they stymie growth and hinder healing.

The legitimate pain of honestly dealing with missed blessings can lead to healing and life. Trying to avoid this legitimate pain just piles layers of illegitimate pain on top of it.

People who procrastinate coming to grips with their past often reap harvests of guilt, anguish, and remorse. Their pain multiplies and sorrows double because they did not choose the legitimate pain that comes with facing the truth.

A certain amount of pain is a given when you live with other human beings. But you have a choice about the kind of pain you experience—the legitimate pain of real problems or the illegitimate pain of trying to cover them up.

The diviners . . . tell false dreams;
they comfort in vain.
—ZECH. 10:2

Dean's emotional problems had worsened for ten years—since he had been involved in a car accident at age eleven. His belligerent outbursts had alienated his friends and strained his family. But Dean's mother refused to acknowledge how serious it had become. She insisted he would get better, that their life would eventually be like it was back "in Michigan," before the family moved to Texas, before the accident, before Dean's problems began. Then came retirement. Dean's parents planned to move to the mountains, and all the children approved—except Dean. When he saw the "For Sale" sign in the yard, he overturned chairs, smashed lamps, and cut family photos to shreds. This last hostile act broke his mother's heart. From baby pictures to recent family portraits, each was torn beyond repair. As she gathered the shreds of her past, she was forced to realize that even if Dean recovered, their lives would never again be like they had been "in Michigan."

Like sorcerers who "tell false dreams," denying reality provides vain comfort—and space for problems to escalate.

> *You desire truth in the inward parts,*
> *And in the hidden part You will make me to know*
> *wisdom.*
> —PS. 51:6

When Greg first heard about the family blessing, he immediately remembered being four years old, waiting for his mother to bring a new baby home from the hospital. To his surprise, she brought home *two* babies—and his life was never the same. Greg loved his twin sisters, but he still had to share his parents' time and attention with two newcomers. People still cooed about the cute twins, barely noticing their older brother. And the girls enjoyed a special closeness brother Greg just couldn't share.

Years later, Greg noticed a nagging insecurity in his life that traced directly back to the twins' arrival. So the next time the family gathered, Greg mustered his courage and gently brought up the subject. To his astonishment, his family cried. "I always thought it might have bothered you," his mother said, "but I didn't know what to say." Greg, Mom, Dad, and the twins all talked and reaffirmed their love. Any nagging guilt over the situation was now resolved and turned into gratitude for Greg's courage and honesty.

Bitterness and resentment flourish in the musty closet—but healing requires fresh air.

Let not mercy and truth forsake you;
Bind them around your neck,
Write them on the tablet of your heart.
—PROV. 3:3

One of the funniest faces on the silver screen belongs to comedian Jim Varney, who has starred in several films and a hilarious series of commercials for various products. He plays Ernest P. Worrell, an incredibly clumsy "hick" who is constantly pestering his pal, Vern. Whenever he wants Vern to remember something really important (like the particular product he is endorsing), Ernest tells him, "Tattoo that on your brain, Vern."

We hope you will "tattoo on your brain" this principle and write "on the tablet of your heart": *In the vast majority of cases, people who do not give the blessing never received it themselves.* Our second recommendation for living without a blessing is based on this tattooed message: Understand as much as you can about your parents' background.

How much do you know about the "climate of blessing" in your parents' home when they were growing up?

> *Understanding is a wellspring of life to him who has it.*
> —PROV. 16:22

Andrea came home from the singles retreat feeling very unblessed. Besides an occasional hug, her father had never demonstrated any of the five elements of the blessing she had just learned about. So Andrea took the first opportunity she could to talk to her father about his past. He told her he had grown up in a well-to-do English family. His parents, who had died before Andrea was born, had raised their only son with all the dignity and care afforded any English citizen of high birth. A nanny cared for him, while his parents kept the respectable distance proper for teaching children discipline and manners. He called his father "Sir"—not "Dad" or "Daddy." Meaningful touching was strictly taboo, and words of praise were rare.

In one hour, Andrea learned more about her father than she had in the nineteen previous years, and she gained a new understanding of his actions. From his perspective, he was almost a fanatic at insuring that his children received the blessing. And all the time she had thought he was withholding it!

Understanding is the wellspring of life because it paves the way for restoration.

Say to wisdom, "You are my sister,"
And call understanding your nearest kin.
—PROV. 7:4

To better understand the kind of home which shaped your own parents (or other care givers), take a few moments to compile what you know about that home. (If you don't know the answers, and your parents are still living, ask them!)

Take your mother, for instance. Was she raised in an intact home? Did one of her parents die early or leave? Was there sickness in the family? How old were her parents when she was born? Did she have brothers and sisters? What was the cultural and religious climate of the home? What was the family's source of income, and how adequate was it? What major world events took place while she was a child that might have affected her (the Great Depression? the Vietnam War?)?

You might even construct a short biography of each parent's life. Be as objective as possible in order to get a clear picture and better understanding.

If you can, pray over the person whose portrait you have put together. Think of that person not as your parent, but as someone who hungered for the blessing and may not have received it.

> *But may the God of all grace, who called us to His*
> *eternal glory by Christ Jesus, after you have*
> *suffered a while, perfect, establish, strengthen, and*
> *settle you.*   —1 PETER 5:10

Honesty and understanding are helpful first steps in learning to cope with a blessing deficit. But facing the fact that a blessing was missing doesn't erase the loneliness and low self-esteem of feeling unblessed. And understanding that parents were doing their best can foster forgiveness or reconciliation, but it still doesn't restore a missing blessing.

Besides honesty and understanding, a person who has missed the blessing needs *healing*—healing from the One who is the Source of all blessings. Facing the problem honestly and opening the mind to understanding helps clear the way for God to start healing—perfecting, establishing, strengthening, settling; filling an empty soul with blessing and then using that soul to bless others.

_____

Today, thank God for the blessings He wants to give to you and through you. Pledge to Him as much honesty and openheartedness as you can muster, then trust Him to do the rest.

Oh, satisfy us early with Your mercy,
That we may rejoice and be glad all our days!
—PS. 90:14

Through God's grace, missing blessings can be restored. But how much better to "satisfy" children "early" by blessing them every day, as the parents did in these children's lives:

1. My parents didn't compare my abilities with those of other kids, but helped me see my unique value.
2. My parents let me give back to them when I got older, like picking up the tab at dinner.
3. I appreciated my father working to keep a good relationship with me when I was a teenager. That helped keep me from some bad dating relationships.
4. When I asked for it, my mother would give me advice on dating and other areas of my life.
5. I always had the best sack lunch of anybody in my class.
6. My folks were always willing to help me work through conflicts with my friends.
7. My father went with me when I had to take back an ugly dress a saleswoman had talked me into buying.

Everyday blessings take time, commitment, and planning. How can you more effectively build them into a child's life?

That we may be able to comfort those who are in
any trouble, with the comfort with which we
ourselves are comforted by God. —2 COR. 1:4

Healing rarely occurs overnight. Instantaneous healings do happen, but a gradual restoration is more common. Sprained ankles or broken arms need time to be as good as new. The same is true of the heart that has been denied the blessing. Complete healing will probably take time—perhaps more time than it takes to finish working through this book. If the pain is deep, professional help may be a godsend.

But God *has* promised "health and healing" to those who depend on Him. And life doesn't have to stand still while that healing is taking place. People recovering from an injury are usually up and around long before the wound has completely healed—they may even find themselves helping doctors and nurses care for other patients. That's a good picture to keep in mind during a "blessings convalescence." You don't have to be completely healed to give blessings to others. In fact, the act of blessing is good therapy for people mending from hurt relationships.

One of the best ways to speed healing is to "help the Doctor" by blessing others.

You are cursed with a curse.
—MAL. 3:9

Every night, Helen would stay at the library as long as she could, hoping her father would have passed out from drinking by the time she got home. Too often, however, he was awake and in front of the television set when she came home.

"Come give your father a hug," he would say when Helen tried to sneak in. Then his "fun" would begin. Always careful not to leave "marks that show on the outside," every day he left heart-wrenching scars on Helen's soul.

People like Helen often have trouble even relating to the concept of a family blessing. From their perspective, they have not just missed a blessing from their mother or father; they have actually received a curse! Can such people ever move past this hurt and pain toward the healing of feeling loved and accepted? If you had asked Helen this question four years ago, her answer would have been an emphatic no. And Helen still struggles with her past at times, but now she would answer the question "Is there hope?" with a resounding yes. She has hope in God, who has always provided help to people cursed by the crushing words or actions of others.

How would you distinguish between "not being blessed" and "being cursed"? How would the consequences in a child's life be different?

> *Nevertheless the LORD your God would not listen to*
> *Balaam, but the LORD your God turned the curse*
> *into a blessing for you, because the LORD your God*
> *loves you.*
> —DEUT. 23:5

Balaam, a sorcerer in the ancient Near East, was greatly respected by the pagan kings in the area. When the nation of Israel camped just outside the Promised Land, this worried one king named Balak. In fear and desperation, he sent for Balaam to come and curse God's people so he could defeat them in battle.

The *curse* is translated from the Hebrew word *qelalah,* which means "to esteem lightly, to dishonor."* (This word is used of a "scanty" meal or a "trickle" of water.) It referred to something to be despised, or that was not of high value. In Old Testament times, and even today, when we curse people, we devalue them. We take someone who is valuable and worthy of honor and blessing—like God's people in Balaam's time and each of His children today—and we place a value on them that is far below their actual worth.

But God did not want that to happen to His people. He took that curse of Balaam's and turned it into a blessing for His people instead.

A third step in learning to live without the family blessing is realizing that God can—and wants to—turn even curses into blessing.

*Hebrew Lexicon, p. 866.

*Behold, I stand at the door and knock. If anyone
hears My voice and opens the door, I will come in
to him and dine with him, and he with Me.*

—REV. 3:20

Some children will never, in this life, hear words of
love or acceptance from their parents. The parents
may be dead or out of touch. Or they may be so far
gone in their own pain or selfishness that they are in-
capable of meeting their children's needs.

In some cases, the relationship may have deterio-
rated to the point that a blessing couldn't get through
even if both parties wanted it to. Whatever the reason,
the children of such parents have to face the fact that
if they wait for their mother or father to bless them,
they will wait forever.

But God doesn't want anyone to wait that long. Remember Helen? When she finally faced facts about her
blessing and turned to listen to the voice of her heavenly Father calling her, she discovered an open door
of blessing. She found a spiritual family blessing that
provided her with every element she had missed in
her home.

*All children—blessed or unblessed, small or grown—can find love
and acceptance in God's spiritual family blessing.*

God sets the solitary in families;
He brings out those who are bound into prosperity.
—PS. 68:6

Practically speaking, how does "God's spiritual family blessing" happen in a person's life? How are relational curses reversed and blessing deficits compensated? Simply put, God provides the family blessing by putting us in a wonderful new spiritual family!

First of all, *God blesses us by being our heavenly Parent.* Unlike our earthly parents, His blessing is full, dependable, and eternal. And He communicates it to us through His Word, through the whisper of His Holy Spirit, and through the actions of other people.

That brings us to the second channel of the spiritual family blessing: God blesses us by giving us *a whole new set of earthly fathers, mothers, brothers, and sisters* who nurture us, help us heal, encourage us to grow, and teach us how to bless others. The church is one of His most important channels of blessing.

Whether or not your physical family blessed you, God has put you in a spiritual family where you can receive a prosperity of blessings.

For He Himself has said, "I will never leave you nor forsake you." So we may boldly say,

> *"The LORD is my helper;*
> *I will not fear.*
> *What can man do to me?"*
> —HEB. 13:5–6

Helen was never secure in her relationship with her father. The first thing she worried about when she came home at night was what kind of mood he would be in. One night he would be furious and abusive. The next night he would seem indifferent. Occasionally he could even be very nice. These vacillations kept Helen off balance and left her insecure and questioning herself.

Yet when Helen trusted Jesus Christ as her Lord and Savior, she found she had a source of blessing to be with her each day of her life and beyond! She had a heavenly Father who would never desert her or forsake her or abuse her. She could go about her life in confidence.

When we have a personal relationship with Jesus Christ, our spiritual parentage is secure. This is true no matter how secure our relationship is with our earthly parents.

Regardless of our earthly parents, we can find security in the dependable and everlasting love of our heavenly Father.

> *As one whom his mother comforts,*
> *so I will comfort you.*
> —ISA. 66:13

Helen's mother was never around during those evenings when her father was drunk and abusive. True, her mother worked nights, but she wasn't around much in the day, either. She was so frightened of having to live on her own that she turned a blind eye to her daughter's horror. Instead of being a source of comfort, she, too, was a source of pain. Helen grew up thinking that being held and comforted was a luxury she just couldn't afford. Imagine Helen's joy to learn that God is not only a dependable Father but a tender, nurturing Mother. He cares for us faithfully, guides us gently, and worries over us when we stray. Realizing that her heavenly Parent was not only dependable, but present to comfort her in her pain helped Helen relax her defenses and open herself to new love.

Regardless of what our earthly parents did, we can find comfort in the nurturing, motherly arms of God.

Now all who believed were together. . . . continuing daily with one accord in the temple, and breaking bread from house to house. —ACTS 2:44,46

Remember the frightened little girl who needed "someone with skin on" to hug her? Our heavenly Father knows all about our need for physical companionship to build our lives and encourage us. That is why when we accept Christ, we gain not only a secure and comforting relationship with our heavenly Parent, but also an entire family of brothers and sisters in Christ— men and women "with skin on" who can communicate God's love, wisdom, and blessing to us!

The early church provided a very good model to follow. They were often in each other's homes (the earliest churches started in homes) and shared meals together. They were literally a family of the faith—related not by physical birth, but by spiritual birth. They all shared the same heavenly Father, and they were all necessary members of one another.

God's family is His way of providing a blessing "with skin on."

> *Exhort him as a father, younger men as brothers,*
> *the older women as mothers, the younger women*
> *as sisters, with all purity.*
> —1 TIM. 5:1–2

God often uses members of the family of faith to fill major "blessing gaps" in a person's life. For instance, I (Gary) was in college when my father died, leaving a huge vacuum in my life. At this crossroads period, a godly man named Rod Toews stepped in. Rod could have easily let his busy schedule crowd out time for a hurting collegian. But Rod attached high value to me and took me under his wing to shepherd and support. Both verbally and by his presence, Rob gave me the blessing now missing in my life.

I (John) was a freshman in high school when I met Doug Barram, a Young Life area director. He had come to watch a freshman football game. Now, besides a few dedicated parents, *nobody* goes to freshman football games. Yet Doug was there, offering words of encouragement to a young man who had not yet heard about Christ. Over the next few years, this man took a fatherly interest in me and my brothers, providing spiritual support to three boys from a single-parent home. Each of us eventually came to know Christ because this man's deep love for his Savior was reflected in his fatherly love for us.

Is God calling you to fill in a blessing gap in someone's life?

Yes, I have loved you with an everlasting love;
therefore with lovingkindness I have drawn you.
                                                    —JER. 31:3

Helen worked in the accounting department for a major oil company. There, she met Karen, a committed Christian, who had prayed for the opportunity to share God's love with someone at the office. At first, Karen was a mystery to Helen. She seemed to have such a positive attitude and such a calm spirit—even when the pressure was on at work. Karen's inner peace and lack of anxiety made Helen want to be around her.

Soon, Karen and Helen had struck up a friendship and were sharing stories about the rigors of dating and their frustrations at work. But Karen also began sharing with Helen the good news about a heavenly Father Helen could come to know.

At first, Helen didn't want anything to do with such talk. She had experienced enough of fathers to last a lifetime. Yet gradually, in spite of herself, the Holy Spirit working through Karen's life drew Helen to a saving knowledge of Christ and a healing source of blessing for her life.

God uses members of the family of faith to draw others to Him and pass along His blessings.

> *We have blessed you from the house of the LORD.*
> —PS. 118:26

Karen took Helen to church with her for the first time in Helen's adult life. Helen couldn't believe what happened. She was asked to stand up as a visitor and was greeted by the pastor. After church, a number of people told her they were glad she had come. One elderly lady even hugged her! Helen went with Karen to the singles Sunday school class. People shared prayer requests before a short message, and they actually held hands and prayed for each other.

Helen found people who had never laid eyes on her treating her like a sister and encouraging her to come again. For the first time, Helen experienced the blessing a church family could be, and God used that experience to change her life.

When we have a secure personal relationship with a heavenly Father, and a spiritual family that offers warmth, love, and acceptance, every element of the blessing can overflow in our lives.

So we, being many, are one body in Christ, and individually members of one another.

—ROM. 12:5

Just in case you have forgotten, let's review the five elements of the blessing: (1) meaningful touch; (2) a spoken message; (3) attaching high value; (4) picturing a special future; (5) active commitment to see the blessing come to pass.

Karen saw that Helen received each element of the blessing, and it brought Helen to the Savior and to His church. By introducing her friend to a loving church family, Karen was able to see her blessing multiplied as many people took an interest in Helen's life.

God has equipped the church, the local body of believers, to provide each aspect of the blessing to people in need. Where churches are growing and thriving, you will find a body of believers who are practicing the five elements of the blessing. These churches also draw in the unsaved, instead of simply luring other believers away from the church down the street.

Are you firmly planted in a congregation where you are blessed and empowered to bless others? If not, what can you do about it?

> *And may the Lord make you increase and abound*
> *in love to one another and to all.*
> —1 THESS. 3:12

A three-year period brought tremendous changes for Helen. She had grown from feeling isolated and alone to feeling truly blessed for the first time in her life. Helen could retire now in the shelter of her caring friends at church and forget all about the past, right?

Not quite.

Helen had eaten fully from the feast of life God had provided in His blessing. Now she needed to become a source of blessing to others around her. For the first time, she could think of people in the office and at her apartment building in terms of what she could give, not just what she needed from them. Because her life was filled with God's blessing through His Spirit and His people, she could love and serve them without needing a response.

Blessing is a stream that flows through us, not a stagnant pool that ends with us.

*Now to Him who is able to do exceedingly
abundantly above all that we ask or think,
according to the power that works in us, to Him be
glory in the church by Christ Jesus to all
generations.*

—EPH. 3:20–21

Helen tried hard to be a source of blessing to her friends at church and work, but she had one final challenge. As incredible as it seemed, Helen also needed to become a source of blessing to her father—the one who had caused her so much pain.

"Couldn't I just skip this part?" Helen asked her pastor. Yet in her heart she knew she would never be truly free of his grip over her life until she could do this.

Later, we will discover how Helen approached her first meeting with her father in years. It was the second most meaningful day in her life. Her most meaningful day was when she met the Lord Jesus, the One who blessed her more than she ever thought possible.

Jesus can change your life, or the lives of loved ones who are struggling without the blessing, by providing God's spiritual family blessing and thus enriching relationship with your children, parents, spouse, friends, and church family.

> *Therefore be patient. . . . See how the farmer waits*
> *for the precious fruit of the earth, waiting patiently*
> *for it until it receives the early and latter rain. You*
> *also be patient. Establish your hearts.*
> —JAMES 5:7–8

One more word for those who have missed a blessing and those who care about them (that should include just about everybody!). Note James's gentle reminder about patience.

Growth comes in God's good time. If we faithfully plant seeds of love and acceptance, the harvest will grow. And in the meantime, we have the care of other people and God's Holy Spirit to guide and sustain us.

But patience doesn't just mean "toughing it out." Patience doesn't mean stoic cynicism or bitter resignation. That would be like the patient farmer deciding just to wait and see whether grain will grow out of the hard, weed-choked ground! Instead, healthy patience requires us to make up our minds—establish our hearts—and do whatever we can to prepare for God's work in our lives. Then we can wait in confidence, knowing that God will do His part.

Pray for patience and the ability to trust God's promises of blessing to those who wait on Him.

> *But Esau ran to meet him, and embraced him, and*
> *fell on his neck and kissed him, and they wept. . . .*
> *And Jacob said, . . . "Please, take my blessing that*
> *is brought to you, because God has dealt graciously*
> *with me, and because I have enough."*
> —GEN. 33:4,10–11

What a glorious happy ending for a story of deceit and disappointment! The last time we saw Esau (at the beginning of the year), he was giving a "great and bitter cry" because his brother, Jacob, had tricked him out of his blessing—and Jacob was slinking out of the country so Esau couldn't kill him. Now, twenty years later, the two brothers embrace with tears—and Jacob wants to give Esau back his blessing in the form of generous gifts.

Whether Jacob could actually give Esau back his lost blessing is beside the point. This scripture shows us an exciting picture of forgiveness, restoration, and growth. In the time they were apart, Jacob had changed from an ambitious, driven person to a wise, secure patriarch. Esau had somehow come to terms with his loss and his anger and had learned to forgive. They sought each other. Their relationship was restored. As far as we know, they lived in peace the rest of their lives.

In God's grace, even stories of missed blessings can have happy endings.

> *Let the husband render to his wife the affection due
> her, and likewise also the wife to her husband.*
> —1 COR. 7:3

Early in our research on the blessing, we went
through this material with several couples in a Bible
study group. We asked for the participants' honest
evaluation of the material during the sessions, and they
filled out a written evaluation at the end.

One of our favorite comments was written by a wife
in the group. Commenting on what her husband had
learned during the class, she wrote, "Dennis has
learned so much about how to bless the children. It has
made a real difference in his relationship with them.
How about teaching him how to bless me!"

Her request was right on target. As we have seen,
the elements of the blessing rest in the heart of *any*
healthy relationship, especially that of husband and
wife. In the next few weeks, therefore, we will explore
how we can apply the five elements of the blessing in
the marriage relationship. Don't take a vacation if
you're not married! Instead, focus on how you can
apply the daily scriptural truths to your most vital relationships.

---

*Giving the blessing to your mate (or any significant person in your
life) is an active way to give him or her "the affection due."*

*Be tenderhearted . . . not returning evil for evil or
reviling for reviling, but on the contrary
blessing . . . that you may inherit a blessing.*
—1 PETER 3:8–9

Laura couldn't believe the pastor's words! After listening carefully to her valid complaints about her husband, he had gently asked, "Laura, have you ever forgiven him for his many faults?"

Of course she had not forgiven him. He had caused her suffering, and she wasn't going to let him off the hook that easily. But sometime during the next week, as she thought about the pastor's advice, Laura began to realize *she* was the one on the hook. (Her husband certainly wasn't losing any sleep about his behavior!) After meeting with the pastor again, Laura gave her life to Christ. Then she chose to forfeit her need for revenge, to forgive her husband for all he had done, and to learn to love him unconditionally.

When Laura's truck driver husband returned home that weekend, he thought he had entered the wrong house! Just the week before, everything he did made his wife mad; now she was going out of her way to do things for him. Five months later he, too, made an appointment with the pastor. "Laura's changed so much," he said. "It's made me realize what a rotten husband I am. Do you think you can help me?"

---

*Making the decision to bless your mate "no matter what" can reap
unexpected benefits in your marriage.*

> *Beloved, if God so loved us, we also ought to love*
> *one another.*
> —1 JOHN 4:11

How did Laura bless her husband? When Laura's life was changed by Christ, she could, out of the overflow of her life, attach high value to him and bless him. For instance, instead of nagging him to quit truck driving and get another job, she found ways to encourage him. She took advantage of his absences to take care of her everyday business so she would have time for him when he was home. Before, she had gone days without speaking to him when she was angry. Now, she shared her feelings, but without anger and hate. Meaningful touch even re-entered their relationship, something Laura had withheld from her husband when her spirit was unforgiving and bitter.

Granted, this is a dramatic example of what can happen when one spouse decides to be a source of blessing. However, in almost any marriage, providing the elements of the blessing to a spouse can encourage and rejuvenate the relationship.

Show us a couple that is growing together, and we'll show you two people practicing these principles of blessing.

*"A man shall . . . be joined to his wife, and the two
shall become one flesh." This is a great mystery, but
I speak concerning Christ and the church.*
—EPH. 5:31–32

The same five elements that make the blessing effective in any relationship will strengthen and deepen a marriage. The element of meaningful touch, for example, is vital to a healthy marriage—the physical expression of intimacy that makes a man and a woman "one flesh."

Sexual touching is a beautiful and powerful facet of meaningful touch in marriage. At its best, the sexual relationship between husband and wife is a joyful expression of closeness, mutual acceptance, and delight in each other—perhaps the most intense form of intimacy two human beings can experience.

In fact, as Cliff and Joyce Penner remind us, the Bible uses the sexual relationship between husband and wife as the symbol of the relationship between Christ and the church. "In this intense fusion of body, emotion, and spirit with another, we experience a glimpse of the relationship that God would like to have with us—the total giving of ourselves to Him. This elevates the sexual relationship to the level of a sacrament."*

Sexual touching is one way a husband and wife bless each other in marriage.

*Joyce J. Penner and Clifford L. Penner, *Counseling for Sexual Disorders*, Resources for Christian Counseling (Dallas: Word, 1990).

> *Live joyfully with the wife [or husband] whom you love.*
> —ECCL. 9:9

Sexual intimacy is not the only important kind of meaningful touch in a marriage, of course. Dr. Kevin Lehman, in his book, *Sex Begins in the Kitchen*, reminds us that genuine intimacy is developed through many small acts of touching—hugging in the kitchen, holding hands at the mall, or snuggling close on the sofa watching television.

It's always a good idea to look before you hug, though. A red-faced seminar participant told us what happened when he tried to give this part of the blessing to his wife. One afternoon after cutting the grass, he came in to take a shower. He left the bathroom door open, and as he walked to the rack to get a towel, he saw his wife in the kitchen preparing dinner. *What a time for meaningful touching,* he thought. He ran down the hall in his birthday suit and burst into the kitchen to give his wife a big hug. What he hadn't seen from the bathroom was his neighbor's wife, who had come to visit and saw more of him than she ever expected! His timing was terrible, but no one could fault his commitment to meaningfully touch his wife!

Make a list of ways you can work meaningful touch into your marriage outside of the bedroom.

Set me as a seal upon your heart,
as a seal upon your arm;
for love is as strong as death.
—SONG 8:6

Meaningful touch communicates so much in a marriage: acceptance, affection, even ongoing commitment. One wise husband, Art, realized the importance of this need during a difficult time for his wife. Marilyn was in the hospital, recovering from a radical mastectomy. Art realized she was feeling insecure about whether he would still find her attractive.

On the morning she was to be released, Art took her hand and told her, "Sugar, I want you to know that you're as beautiful to me now as you were on our wedding night." Then he added, "After you get home and get rested up, we're going to have to get the lock fixed on the bedroom door."

Tears of understanding sprang up in Marilyn's eyes. Early in their marriage, one of the boys had walked into their room at an inappropriate time. "We're going to have to get the lock fixed" had became their private password to an intimate evening. Art's words and actions that morning were his way of assuring her that this important element of the blessing would still be a part of their relationship.

Meaningful touch can be a powerful expression of commitment in marriage.

> *Speak evil of no one . . . be peaceable, gentle,*
> *showing all humility to all men.* —TITUS 3:2

The second element of the blessing—a spoken message—tends to fall by the wayside in the daily routine of marriage. Husbands, especially, are often accused of neglecting this part of the blessing, but wives also fail to speak words of affirmation and respect: "I'm proud of you!" "You did a great job with that account!" "Thank you for helping me get that done so quickly!" "You look wonderful!"

Of course, *refraining* from certain kinds of speech is also a vital part of blessing our mate. Not only do we make a point of speaking affirming words of acceptance, but we bite back words that attack, devalue, and belittle. "You're hopeless!" "What a stupid thing to do!" "I can't ever count on you!"

This doesn't mean we should be dishonest or avoid touchy areas of conversation. We can be honest and even confrontational without wounding each other with words. The key is using all our words to build bridges, not walls, between us.

Blessing our spouse includes speaking words of blessing and not speaking words of curse.

Pleasant words are like a honeycomb,
Sweetness to the soul and health to the bones.
—PROV. 16:24

A popular bumper sticker slogan reads, "Have you hugged your kids today?" Another equally important phrase you can copy and paste to your refrigerator, bathroom mirror, or forehead is: "Have you praised your mate today?" An everyday dose of praise, even a simple statement like "Great dinner, Honey" or a "You are so kind" or "I think you handled that little problem just right" sweetens a relationship. Such words of praise actually combine two elements of the blessing. They involve a spoken message, and they express high value.

Why not try a project to discover the difference words of praise can make? Each day for thirty days, make a point to praise at least one thing you appreciate about your spouse each day. Be sure you point out character traits (kindness, punctuality, generosity) as well as accomplishments. And don't tell your husband or wife you're doing this. We give this assignment to many couples in counseling, and it in itself has caused positive changes in relationships.

To get started, write out a specific statement of praise for your mate and a specific time (breakfast, bedtime) to share it. Then, follow through to add "sweetness" and "health" to your marriage.

With what parable shall we picture it?
—MARK 4:30

As we have seen, word pictures are wonderful tools to help us communicate messages of high value. This applies for a mate as well as for our children.

The most effective word pictures, remember, use a common object to illustrate a feeling. One creative husband used a bottle of correcting fluid as a word picture to praise his wife.

"Sweetheart," this man said, "you remind me of this little bottle of 'White Out.' Every time I make a mistake or do something to hurt you, you cover over my faults with your love. Every day, you let me start with a clean sheet of paper—and I love you for it."

Don't underestimate the power of such pictures! They leave a positive impression on the one you love.

What qualities do you most value in your mate? Make a short list of ordinary objects that remind you of those qualities. This list can be a good starting point for a winning word picture.

My lips shall greatly rejoice when I sing to You,
And my soul, which You have redeemed.
—PS. 71:23

One woman sent us a moving word picture she prepared to thank her husband for his love:

There was once an beautiful oak vanity—shiny and beautifully made. Over the years, however, it lost its shine and got nicked up a bit, and the owners finally stored it in the basement with other long-forgotten items. One day a woodworker came along and noticed the vanity. The owner said, "That old piece of junk? It isn't worth the wood it's made of." But the persistent craftsman thought otherwise. With a sense of pride in his soon-to-be masterpiece, he took the vanity home and began to work. He stripped off the old varnish and stain, buffed every nick from the surface, and carefully re-stained it. Finally, he sealed all his loving work with a shining coat of lacquer.

I am that beat-up old vanity, and you are the craftsman. Because of your love and caring persistence, I am in the process of being refurbished—better than new! Thank you for not allowing me to be destroyed by time, but for recognizing my real potential and helping me develop it.

This beautiful word picture also pictures God's persistent and redeeming love. Thank Him!

You shall teach them diligently to your children.
—DEUT. 6:7

These examples of everyday blessing, shared by many of our friends, can teach children to have healing relationships by instilling self-confidence and modeling love:

1. My mother was always interested in what I was doing at school, but she wasn't interfering.
2. My father acted more excited about getting to spend time with us kids than he did about working at the office.
3. My father helped me buy an old Mustang that had been wrecked and helped me rebuild it into a beautiful car.
4. I never felt like I had to perform to gain my father's approval.
5. Some people's parents criticize them behind their backs, but my parents' friends always told me positive words my parents had said about me.
6. My mother had Bible study with me every Monday morning before I went to school.
7. I didn't appreciate it at the time, but I know that my parents protected me by setting a curfew during my dating years.

Pray that the blessing you give to children will help prepare them to bless a future husband or wife abundantly.

The entrance of Your words gives light;
It gives understanding.
—PS. 119:130

Today's verse specifically applies to the words of God, but also reveals the clarity a good word picture can bring to an issue. Word pictures not only add power to praise; they can also help discuss an important issue or avoid a heated argument. By using a word picture to convey a concern, we often portray a message we can't seem to get across with only words. One woman wrote:

Jake and I get so busy sometimes with our separate careers we rarely have time to talk or just *be* together. I finally told him one day, "Honey, when we take five minutes together to have a cup of tea and just sit quietly, with no one else around, I feel as if I've had a long drink at an oasis in the middle of a desert." We've been making time to be alone together ever since.

Word pictures are a powerful, nonthreatening method for communicating concerns in marriage.

If you have understanding, hear this;
listen to the sound of my words.
—JOB 34:16

Bee's husband, Don, always invited people over for dinner or to stay the night. Bee was also hospitable, but she was tired of cooking for guests in an under-sized kitchen and arranging for ten people to sleep in a house with only two beds. They could easily afford a new home, but Don held back because he didn't want to appear ostentatious. Finally, Bee shared this word picture with him:

"Don, I feel like you're the game warden who takes such good care of the trout in the waterways around our house. Before we were married, I felt like one of those trout, and longed for you to scoop me up in a net and take me to the stream by your house. Then one day you did come for me and gently picked me out of the water—but then you put me in an old, rusty barrel. For twenty-two years you've fed me and kept the water clean. But Don, I still feel like I'm living in a rusty barrel, and I long to swim in the stream!"

Bee's years of longing came to an end that night. Don finally understood how she felt and wrote her a check to hire an architect and begin planning the new house.

Could a word picture help you get across a concern that your mate just can't understand?

*When a man has taken a new wife, he shall not go
out to war or be charged with any business; he
shall be free at home one year, and bring happiness
to his wife whom he has taken.* —DEUT. 24:5

As we have seen, spoken words are an important
way to give our mate the second element of the blessing: attaching high value to him or her. But though important, words lose their meaning unless they are
backed by action. In other words, we need to *show* our
mates how much we value them by behaving in ways
that say, "You matter to me."

Making time to be together is probably the most important "act of high value." It is so important, in fact,
that it was written into codes of law God gave the Hebrew people. The law specified that during the first
year of marriage, a young man should not even have
a job, but should spend all his time getting to know his
wife.

But after that first year, of course, things get tricky.
Jobs eat a lot of time. Kids demand attention. Churches
require involvement. It's easy for husbands and wives
to give each other short shrift in the attention department. When this happens, the message we send may
be "You're important to me, but not as important
as . . . ."

---

*A wise person attaches high value to his or her mate by making time
together a priority. How can you schedule your time to give your mate
higher priority in your marriage?*

Wherever you go, I will go;
and wherever you lodge, I will lodge.
—RUTH 1:16

The fourth element of the blessing, you remember, involves picturing a special future for the one we bless. In the context of marriage, that includes picturing a special future for the two of you together. A marriage thrives on a positive vision of a shared tomorrow.

Several years ago, I watched a television comedy show about an outdoor wedding. In a forest clearing stood the bride with her attendant, the best man, and a worried-looking bridegroom. The minister asked the bride to say her vows, which she had written especially for this occasion. She launched into goal after goal, commitment after commitment, dream after dream. In fact, she went on so long that night fell in the forest.

When she finally finished, the exhausted minister turned to the groom and asked him to repeat his vows. Looking around nervously, his only words were, "Well, I hope this works out!" His vows were funny, all right, but they were not the kind of words upon which his new bride could build a secure future!

In a marriage, we must let our mate know he or she is a special part of our future.

Therefore let us pursue the things . . . by which one may edify another.
—ROM 14:19

Picturing a special future for those we want to bless also means becoming a student of their lives. That can mean many things in the context of a marriage—involving ourselves in that person's life, sharing interests, providing encouragement for growth. But another important way is to edify that loved one by pointing out the good qualities that even they cannot see. When we do that, we help bring out the best in that person.

April was a lively, outgoing girl with a serious, overly-organized big brother. In contrast, she always considered herself flighty, irresponsible, and disorganized. Fortunately, she married a man who proved a sensitive student of his wife. He changed both her self-image and her life the day he opened the kitchen cabinets and pointed out that "flighty, irresponsible" people don't hold high-profile jobs or run a household with two small children—they also don't organize the spices alphabetically, as April did!

We bless our mates and picture a special future for them when we help them see their own possibilities.

> Let no corrupt communication proceed out of your
> mouth, but what is good for necessary edification,
> that it may impart grace to the hearers.
>
> —EPH. 4:29

Todd's wife, Betty, was not the world's best house-keeper. And by the time they had three little ones running around, their house was a disaster! Predictably, her husband, Todd, was tidy. He ended up cleaning much of the house himself. But he also spent much of his time berating his wife for her shortcomings. She would *always* be messy, he predicted; she would *never* change. He even spun scenarios of their grandchildren's catching incurable diseases and the Health Department's shutting them down.

Not only was Todd not placing high value on his wife; he was making the very thing he sought to change become a lasting part of their future! By painting a picture of his wife with no window of hope or door for change, he boxed her into viewing herself as the "world's worst housekeeper."

Picturing a special future for our mate means leaving room for positive change in the future instead of boxing them in with negative predictions.

Anxiety in the heart . . . causes depression;
But a good word makes it glad.
—PROV. 12:25

Remember Todd, who thought his messy wife would never change? His story has a happy ending. In a Sunday school class, Todd saw for the first time how his words of a negative future had hurt his wife instead of helped her. He learned that he was killing any motivation his wife had to change. Whenever she would try to make a dent in the cleaning chores, he had met her with a "Why can't you keep things like that all the time?" His negative words communicated to his wife that it was impossible to please him—so why try?

When Todd realized what he was doing, he deliberately stopped criticizing her poor performance and started to praise her efforts. He began sharing his dreams of a house where they could feel comfortable and not embarrassed. And today, even though the house is not up to Todd's immaculate standards, he no longer has to fight his way through laundry in the washroom or fear going into a shower with things growing in it.

_____

Change is slow to take root, but can grow ten times faster in the soil of encouragement than in the hard, rocky soil of criticism.

> *For we are His workmanship, created in Christ*
> *Jesus for good works, which God prepared*
> *beforehand that we should walk in them.*
> —EPH. 2:10

What drives you crazy about your mate? Those extra thirty pounds? Her failure to discipline the children promptly? His unwillingness to share household duties? Her inability to say "I'm sorry"?

Whatever the difficulty, picturing a negative future won't motivate your mate to change. Your mate needs to hear words that picture a special future, positive words that give him or her room to grow into all God can help him or her become.

The question is *how?* How do you come by that vision for a positive future honestly when you can only see problems? Is picturing a special future for your mate simply a form of denial? No, but it may be a matter for prayer! It's hard sometimes to step back and see your husband or wife apart from your own needs and desires. But you may need to do that, in God's strength.

God has a special future in mind for your mate. Ask Him for the grace to share His vision.

Trust in the LORD with all your heart . . .
—PROV. 3:5

You can use this to bless your spouse and envision a special future for the two of you. It's adapted from Proverbs 3:

> Lord, we commit ourselves and our marriage to You. May we trust in You with all our hearts and not lean on our own understanding. But may we seek to know what You would want us to do in all we do. Then You have promised to make our paths straight. May each of us not be wise in our own eyes, but fear You and depart from evil. Let us depend on You to be health to our flesh and strength to our bones. May we honor You with our possessions, and rest in Your promise of plenty.

Pray this prayer every day for a week, letting it soak into your spirit, before sharing it with your spouse. Then, if you like, make it part of a special time you spend together, committing yourselves anew to God, to each other, and to your marriage.

Abhor what is evil. Cling to what is good.
—ROM. 12:9

As we have discovered in earlier meditations, providing the individual elements of the blessing without the glue to hold them all together is not enough. That glue is our active commitment. In fact, this final element of the blessing is at the heart of "cleaving" in a marriage. When the Scriptures tell us we are to "cleave" to our spouse (Gen. 2:24 NASB), the root word in Hebrew means "to cling, to be firmly attached"*—the same idea as "clinging to what is good" in today's verse. The picture is that of being so firmly attached that you cannot be pulled away in one piece!

That firm attachment is not always easy when we deal with fallible, sinful humans—and it's rarely painless. It requires a firm decision to be committed to blessing your spouse, a decision that will not remain intact if you don't make room for your mate's mistakes and failings.

———————

The fifth element of the blessing, active commitment, makes all the other elements work and makes it possible for us to "cleave" to our mate in marriage.

*Hebrew Lexicon, p. 866.

*Put on tender mercies, kindness, humility,
meekness, longsuffering; bearing with one another,
and forgiving one another.*   —COL. 3:12–13

In the 1929 Rose Bowl game, something happened that demonstrated how fallible even a star can be. Roy Riegels was starter and star athlete for the University of California. What actually happened was that Roy made a winning contribution to the *other* team, Georgia Tech. In a brilliant defensive play late in the first half, Roy intercepted a pass, fought off several would-be tacklers, and headed for the end zone and a touchdown. Unfortunately, in fighting off the tacklers, he had gotten turned around and scored a safety for the other team! His mistake put Georgia Tech in front.

At halftime, everyone wondered if Roy's coach, Nibbs Price, would yank him out of the game. No, Roy's name led the starting lineup for the second half. Price had watched Roy work hard all season, and he remained committed to him even when he made a major mistake. Another coach, University of Texas's Darryl Royal, would later express that same kind of active commitment to his players with an old country adage, "You dance with the one who brung ya!"

What these two coaches had, and what every man or woman owes his or her spouse, is the willingness to stay committed, even if the other person fumbles the ball.

*Walk worthy of the calling with which you were
called, with all lowliness and gentleness, with
longsuffering, bearing with one another in love.*
—EPH. 4:1–2

Grant's small manufacturing business had found its
niche in the marketplace and was growing rapidly. But
shortly after he took out a large loan to expand, a mul-
tinational manufacturing concern decided to compete
with Grant's product. They drastically undercut prices
and soon drove Grant out of business. He shut down
his plant and liquidated his equipment. He lost his
home, and his children had to change schools midyear.
Devastated over these developments, Grant contem-
plated suicide, but one thing held him back:

I didn't know the Lord when my business went under,
and my whole world seemed to end. The one thing that
kept me from suicide was my wife, Amy, and the way she
constantly believed in me and blessed me with her love.
Listening to her pray for me at night and having her hold
me and let me cry pulled me through. I tell everyone she
saved my life twice—when the business failed and when
she led me to Jesus Christ.

*"Bearing with one another in love" is the essence of active commit-
ment in a marriage.*

In this the love of God was manifested toward us,
that God has sent His only begotten Son into the
world, that we might live through Him.
—1 JOHN 4:9

Chances are, at some point in your marriage, your mate will (or has already) hurt you deeply, let you down, not come through for you. And chances are you will do (or have already done) the same to your mate.

Every husband or wife occasionally drops the ball and proves fallible. That's why, if we are to be people of blessing, our commitment to our mate must rest on our decision to love him or her in spite of failures and faults. Our love must be the kind of love that motivated our heavenly Father to bless us with his Son, despite the fact that we didn't deserve it.

Only in that love, which we soak up from the Father, can we cope with our disappointments and our guilt and keep loving "in spite of."

Heavenly Father, teach me to love as You love—in spite of faults.

*Be kindly affectionate to one another with brotherly
love, in honor giving preference to one another.*
—ROM. 12:10

Earlier this year, we talked about setting aside a special evening to provide a child with all the elements
of the blessing. The same idea works beautifully for
blessing a husband or wife. You can plan a memorable
evening for your spouse that will help him or her experience your honor in a new way. A wedding anniver-
sary is always a good time for this, but any evening
away from the children and the phone will do. It
doesn't even have to be an evening. One husband actually gave a "Morning of Blessing" for his wife, including breakfast in bed.

Privacy is your most important consideration for
this special time together; you want to focus on your
spouse with no interruptions. If finances permit, you
might want to rent a hotel room for the night. Or swap
houses with close friends for the night (leave your kids
for them to baby-sit and promise to do the same for
them sometime). Be creative in finding ways to cut the
cost down and still have the privacy to really focus on
each other.

*You can waste precious time on a thousand different things, but you
will never waste one minute when you're blessing your mate.*

He brought me to the banqueting house,
and his banner over me was love.
—SONG 2:4

What should you do during your special evening together? A special meal is a great start. Afterwards, use
your creativity to communicate your love and commitment. Write a "story of our marriage" or make a tape
recording of your fond memories. Enjoy looking at
photographs of your special times together. Share a
word picture you have created or a list of ten reasons
why you would again choose your spouse to be your
life partner. One great way to picture a special future
for your spouse is to dig out your original wedding
vows and repeat them—or write a new set of vows expressing your love and commitment.

If your denomination permits, taking Communion as
you recommit your life to your spouse can be beautiful
and meaningful. Then take an extended time to pray
together, asking God to keep your love fresh and refreshing. And don't forget to touch! Since you've gone
to all the trouble to get away, enjoy each other fully in
the context of renewed love and commitment.

---

*The "banqueting house" doesn't matter as long as the "banner" is
love!*

> *The soul of Jonathan was knit to the soul of David,*
> *and Jonathan loved him as his own soul.*
> —1 SAM. 18:1

We constantly meet people who "wish they had a close friend." Many of those people would not have to make that comment if they knew how to *be* a "close friend." We have discovered in studying the blessing in the Scriptures that an important part of becoming a close friend is applying each element of the blessing in a friendship.

In all the Scriptures, perhaps the most universally acknowledged model of a close friend is Jonathan. His relationship with David is a graduate course in what makes a lasting relationship. These two young men were not a likely pair to strike up a friendship. Jonathan was the heir apparent to his father's throne and a mighty warrior in his own right. He and David first met just after David killed Goliath. With all the attention David was receiving, Jonathan could have looked at David as a rival and enemy. Yet we are told "Jonathan loved him as his own soul." One reason their friendship was unique is because it was a friend-to-friend relationship that included, and models, every aspect of the blessing.

Of your own friends, whom do you come closest to loving "as your own soul"? What elements make your friendship unique?

And they kissed one another; and they wept together.
—1 SAM. 20:41

Without the fear among men today of expressing appropriate affection, David and Jonathan demonstrated meaningful touching in their friendship. In their last meeting, for instance, when Jonathan had to tell David it was no longer safe for him to be around his father, Saul, the two friends kissed and cried in each other's arms.

For men in our culture, such behavior is almost taboo, but it was not considered strange in ancient Israel, nor is it unusual in many foreign countries. Friends in these cultures demonstrate their love for each other with a kiss or a hug.

Even within the confines of our cultural norms, we can make meaningful touch a part of our blessing to our friends. A touch of the hand, a friendly pat on the back, even a shoulder rub, can convey acceptance and affection. And withholding a hug, or even a handshake, from a friend can freeze that relationship at a surface level.

Dare to reach beyond cultural comfort zones to touch your friends.

> *The LORD be with you as He has been with my father.*
> —1 SAM. 20:13

In giving us another picture of what it means to be a close friend, Jonathan often spoke of his appreciation for David. Even though placed in the awkward position of having to go between his father, Saul, and his friend, David, Jonathan never backed off from his pledge of friendship. He made a verbal covenant with David, promising to be his close companion for life (1 Sam. 20:13). Jonathan spared no words in blessing David.

Some friends thrive on spoken words of blessing, but others feel uncomfortable—especially if the friendship has developed around a shared activity rather than shared words. (Men are especially likely to have such friendships.) But reaching beyond the slight awkwardness of expressing your affection will pay big dividends in terms of a cemented bond of affection.

The next time you reflect on how much you enjoy your friend's company, or how much you miss him when he's not around, or how much you respect and appreciate that person, say so!

The next time you spend time with a friend, speak words of appreciation. If you feel awkward doing so, write a note, sing a song—whatever gets the message across.

*And Jonathan took off the robe that was on him
and gave it to David, with his armor, even to his
sword and his bow and his belt.*   —1 SAM. 18:4

A warrior only lays down his weapons in front of
someone he considers his better. This verse indicates
that Jonathan placed such high value on David that he
sacrificed his symbols of authority (his armor and
robes) to honor his friend.

What kind of actions say "I value our friendship"? In
our hectic society, making the effort to get together—
keeping your appointments and being on time—
speaks volumes. Listening carefully and keeping confi-
dences can tell our friends we treasure them. "Just being there" during times of pain or joy shows high
honor. And of course, we must speak words of high
value to get the message across. Words of support, defense, and praise can all communicate "You are very
important to me."

*What are some practical, specific ways you can show your friends
how much you value your relationship?*

> *May the LORD be between you and me, and*
> *between your descendants and my descendants,*
> *forever."*
>
> —1 SAM. 20:42

These last words Jonathan spoke to David illustrate his active commitment to David and his desire for God to bless David in the future. They express the same sentiment I might convey by putting a hand on your shoulder and saying, "Do whatever you want; I'm not going anywhere."

That doesn't mean all meaningful friendships are lifelong commitments, of course. Although some special relationships do endure the test of time, others flourish for a season and then fade. People move, change, or go on to other things. That's normal.

Expressing active commitment to most friends is not a matter of pledging lifelong intimacy. It's more a matter of saying, "I care about your well-being over the long term and won't desert you just because something else comes up. I'll go where God takes me. But God willing, I won't go anywhere!"

Can you think of a meaningful friendship from your past in which someone's commitment to your well-being helped you grow. Thank God for that person whether or not he or she is still in your life.

Rejoice with those who rejoice, and weep with those who weep.
—ROM. 12:15

Larry was an accomplished "Jonathan" who had many close friends, but he hesitated to reach to his distant, formal boss, Glenn. Larry knew Glenn's teenage son had recently been arrested for selling drugs, and he thought Glenn could use a friend. So he gathered up his courage, walked into Glenn's office, and laid his hand on Glenn's shoulder. "You know, boss," Larry said, "I may be out of line, but you seem to be hurting. I just want you to know if you ever need somebody to talk to, I'm around." Larry expected a curt rebuff. But after a long pause, Glenn looked up. "I'll remember that, Larry. Thanks."

A few days later, the two men met for breakfast. During that meeting, Larry listened while Glenn poured out a heart full of hurt. Larry didn't try to lecture Glenn or talk him out of his pain. In fact, the only time Larry remembered saying more than a sentence or two was when he prayed a short prayer with Glenn in his car. Over the next several months, Larry met every week with Glenn to listen, talk, and pray.

Even those who don't seem friendly can often use a friend.

I thank my God upon every remembrance of you.
—PHIL. 1:3

Glenn, whom we met yesterday, had every reason to thank God for his friend and employee, Larry, because Larry provided him with each element of the blessing. By shaking Glenn's hand or patting him on the back, Larry provided the element of meaningful touch. By pointing out Glenn's positive character traits and praising his attempts to make a fresh start with his wife and children, Larry spoke a blessing and attached high value to Glenn. By giving him the hope of a special future that God could provide regardless of how Glenn's son acted, he pictured a special future. And by committing himself to be available when Glenn needed someone to talk to, he demonstrated active commitment.

Actually, Glenn had *two* things for which to thank the Lord. One was the gift of Larry's friendship. The other was the way his son responded to him as he began to follow Larry's model and become a better friend.

———————

Blessing a friend gives him or her a strong reason for thanksgiving.

It is more blessed to give than to receive.
—Acts 20:35

Who are your true friends? Think about someone in your life who has been an intimate friend. Almost without exception, a close friend will be someone like Jonathan—a man or woman who has demonstrated each aspect of the blessing to you. Such a good friend is truly a gift from God.

But here's another interesting thing about blessing a friend (or anyone else, for that matter): receiving the blessing strengthens our relationship—but giving the blessing strengthens it too. In fact, blessing someone helps us love that person more. Those friends whom we touch meaningfully, honor with our words and actions, and support with our vision and active commitment are usually the friends we love most.

We love the friends who bless us—and the friends we bless!

These things we write to you that your joy may be full.
—1 JOHN 1:4

During this time of year, Christmas cards begin to appear in the stores. If you're an early starter, you may already have gathered your list of friends and started the joyful chore of writing holiday messages.

If you plan to send Christmas cards this year (or even if you hadn't planned on it), why not send a blessing along with your card. You may not be able to physically touch your faraway friends, but you can write a message that tells them how valuable they are and pictures a special year for them. You can pledge your ongoing care and commitment.

If you're the artistic type, you may even want to write and design a card that sends a holiday blessing to all of your friends. Or you may prefer to write a personal holiday letter to a special few, expressing gratitude for their friendship and committing them to the Lord.

The upcoming holiday season is a good to time to think of your faraway friends and to honor them with a blessing.

When he wanted to inherit the blessing, he was rejected.
—HEB. 12:17

The most encouraging place Jim knew of was the bowling alley. He lived for Wednesday nights when he and some guys from work would have a few beers and bowl with a league. To Jim, bowling was a shelter from the troubles he was experiencing in his marriage and in his job as a mechanic.

Then Jim became a Christian. His personal life and his marriage began to change, and he and his wife began attending a large church near their home. But they never seemed to feel comfortable or accepted there. Everyone was polite, but no one greeted them with bright eyes. No one invited them to dinner. And no one seemed to notice when Jim stopped coming to church.

One day, the pastor ran into Jim's wife at the supermarket and innocently asked, "How are you and Jim doing?" She sobbed, "Pastor, Jim won't come back to church. He said he has better friends at the bowling alley than he ever did at church."

The church was designed to be a hotbed of love, friendship, and blessing—so why would someone like Larry find more satisfaction in a bowling alley? Could that happen in your church? (Has it happened to you?)

God . . . [said] to Abraham, "And in your seed all the families of the earth shall be blessed." To you first, God, having raised up His Servant Jesus, sent Him to bless you, in turning away every one of you from your iniquities.
—ACTS 3:25–26

From earliest times, God's people have been called to be a blessing. When God first came to Abraham, He gave a specific promise: "In you all the families of the earth shall be blessed" (Gen. 12:3). Centuries later, in the book of Acts, Peter tells us the form this blessing would take for all nations. The blessing came in the body of the suffering servant, Jesus, a descendant of Abraham's who has the power to bless our lives by freeing us from sin.

Introducing people to Jesus Christ, therefore, is the first and foremost way a church can bless others. When men and women are introduced to the Source of blessing, they come face to face with Someone who can be their best friend and their source of life. Also, within the body of believers, we are called to bless others by supporting their spiritual lives—praying together, studying together, worshiping together.

The church's first priority in blessing others is to introduce them to Christ and help them grow in Christ.

If one member suffers, all the members suffer with it; or if one member is honored, all the members rejoice with it.
                                                    —1 COR. 12:26

The church needs to be, first and foremost, a place where the gospel is preached and Christ is honored as our Lord and Savior. But God also designed the church to be a caring community. When we fail to bless and love our brothers and sisters in Christ, we are failing our duties as a family of God. When one member of the body rejoices, we should all rejoice. When one member weeps, we should all weep.

Sadly, this is not the experience of many people who have gone to church and come away unblessed or lonely. Why is that? The church really doesn't have a shortage of caring people. But many church families don't know how to meet people's relational needs after they come to know Christ and get plugged into the church "system."

The exciting thing about the concept of the blessing is that it can be a guideline for all kinds of loving relationships—with children, husbands and wives, friends. It can also work that way in a church—showing the church how to be a caring community.

The blessing can serve as a guideline for loving relationships within a church family.

October 29 – A CONTAGIOUS BLESSING

A new commandment I give to you, that you love one another. . . . By this all will know that you are My disciples.
—JOHN 13:34–35

If we have been called to provide people with the blessing of knowing Christ, what is the best way to see this happen? The Lord's answer is found in today's verse: We bless others by loving each other. When others see us doing that, they want to know what's going on!

People outside the church will never care how much we know about Christ until they know how much we care for each other. The loving atmosphere in a church committed to blessing is almost irresistible; people are drawn into its fellowship and stay to hear what it's all about. That's why, when a body of believers becomes committed to loving each other, they can truly be called a church that is serious about winning others to Christ and helping them grow.

Love is the contagious secret of a church that gives the blessing to each other and to those outside its fellowship.

*Owe no one anything except to love one another,
for he who loves another has fulfilled the law.*
—ROM. 13:8

Mark was the leader of a large singles Sunday school class. Like many groups, the class struggled with the problems of turnover and building in-depth relationships. But then Mark learned about the blessing. This concept helped transform the class into a source of love and acceptance. Mark gathered a group of people called the Blessing Bunch. They committed themselves to (1) identifying class members who particularly needed one or more elements of the blessing; and (2) meeting those needs.

It wasn't hard to find people in need of a blessing. One class member needed someone to cry with her after she broke up with her boyfriend. Another faced a difficult new assignment at work and needed someone to build his confidence by picturing a special future. Once the Blessing Bunch committed themselves to their mission, needs seemed to come out of the woodwork. Eventually, the principles of the blessing so transformed that group of people that "Have you had your blessing this week?" became the class buzz phrase. Word circulated that Mark's Sunday school class was the place to be if you needed a friend.

What would it take to get a system of "organized blessing" going on in your circle of fellow believers?

And great grace was upon them all.
—ACTS 4:33

Yesterday we saw what happened when a small group in a large singles Sunday school class committed themselves to regularly giving the blessing. But the blessings did not stay confined to that class! As they learned about the blessing, for instance, several members became convicted about their relationships with their parents. One young man even walked out of the classroom and to a pay phone, calling his father for the first time in more than four years. Other people began to share the principles of the blessing with their family members at the church, and healing happened.

The singles class even talked about the concept of the blessing at a Sunday evening service. Mark shared that the married people in the church could bless the singles by not expecting them to get married tomorrow and by inviting them into their homes. This began an "adopt a single" program that helped bring an isolated group into the mainstream of church life.

When just a few people in a church decide to start seriously blessing others, a new sense of warmth and caring can transform the whole body.

Since we are surrounded by so great a cloud of witnesses, let us lay aside every weight, and the sin which so easily ensnares us, and let us run with endurance the race that is set before us, looking unto Jesus, the author and finisher of our faith.
—HEB. 12:1–2

Today is All Saints Day, the day the church has traditionally set aside to honor the great "cloud of witnesses" who have gone before us in the faith. What a wonderful opportunity, as well, to honor those who have blessed our lives.

On this particular day, think of those, living and dead, who have made your life richer and especially those who have helped you know God. For instance, the great-grandmother who raised her family in the faith; the author whose book transformed your life; the teacher who believed in you; the friend who led you to Christ and encouraged you during a "dry" time. How about the men and women of the early church whose faithfulness made your salvation possible?

Today's verse reminds us that no matter how alone we may sometimes feel, we are supported by innumerable others who have loved the Lord and loved well. With such a blessing, how can we not choose to bless others?

Spend today's quiet time in praise and thanksgiving for the blessing of two thousand years of "witnesses."

> *We are bound to thank God always for you,*
> *brethren, as it is fitting, because your faith grows*
> *exceedingly, and the love of every one of you all*
> *abounds toward each other.* —2 THESS. 1:3

Imagine what would happen if an entire church decided to bless those in their fellowship and were trained to do so! This church would be one in which relationship needs were actively met by a welcoming handshake or hug (meaningful touch). People in this church would express appreciation for a fine sermon, work in the children's department, or simply listen to a hurting brother or sister (spoken message). Groups of believers would acknowledge all members' true worth (attaching high value) and give them words of hope and encouragement to reach their God-given potential (a special future). All these elements would be wrapped in the willingness to let people fail and not let them walk away unnoticed, because a decision had been made already that they were valuable (an active commitment).

This church sounds like the kind of church most of us would like to belong to, and it can be. It only takes one person to start a Blessing Bunch that will reach out to others.

———————

If you feel it's appropriate, make a list of people in your church to talk to about starting a Blessing Bunch. In the meantime, pray for an outbreak of "abounding love" in your congregation.

> *Go therefore and make disciples of all the nations,*
> *baptizing them in the name of the Father and of*
> *the Son and of the Holy Spirit, teaching them to*
> *observe all things that I have commanded you; and*
> *lo, I am with you always, even to the end of the*
> *age.*
> —MATT. 28:19

A church committed to applying the principles of the blessing can make a tremendous impact on the unsaved. Once church members experience this concept, they can transport it outside the church walls. Monday through Saturday they can provide the elements of God's blessing to a non-Christian society desperately needing security and acceptance. The blessing can even help us fulfill the Great Commission to "make disciples of all nations."

An employer, for example, can evaluate his or her progress in blessing employees. A schoolteacher who learns about the blessing can recognize the telltale signs of a child's growing up without parental acceptance. A student can befriend a fellow classmate and point him or her toward a secure source of blessing through Christ.

After all, the mark of a disciple is "that you love one another." Applying the principles of the blessing in our daily lives is an effective way to help God's love radiate to a needy world.

What opportunities does your life present for reaching others and "blessing them to Christ"?

> *Therefore we make it our aim . . . to be well*
> *pleasing to Him.*
> —2 COR. 5:9

Must we really be so specific about the principles of the blessing? Can't we just be nice people? If we love God and care about others, won't they automatically feel loved? Maybe, but not always, because so many obstacles stand between a goodwill and the experience of feeling loved and welcome.

We care, but we're committed to being downstairs in five minutes for a meeting. So we say "Good morning" and rush away.

We're concerned, but we don't want to pry. So we say nothing.

We love, but we also feel embarrassed. So we just touch the hand and duck the head.

We want to help, but aren't sure that our motives are pure. So we don't offer assistance.

Aristotle observed, "You stand a far greater chance of hitting the target if you can see it." This statement might not sound too profound, but it is. Churches, parents, spouses, and friends stand a far better chance of hitting the target of loving each other if they can see how to do it.

Following the guidelines provided in the blessing can help our words and actions score a bull's-eye when we want to communicate God's love and acceptance to our loved ones.

For you have found grace in My sight, and I know you by name.
—EX. 33:17

The long-running TV series *Cheers* centers around a group of friends who laugh and cry together at a place "where everybody knows your name." It's pictured as a sort of emotional headquarters where the "regulars" go to share the important issues of their lives—a place where they know they will be accepted. Tragically, regulars also go there to avoid their families, hide from their problems, and "fuel up" for drunken drives across town. This place "where everybody knows your name" is a bar.

Isn't it sad that so many people think a bar is the answer to their need to be known and loved? And doesn't that sad misconception tell us something about what must happen in our churches! After all, would bars be as popular if people thought of church as a place "where everybody knows your name"? And we're not just talking about name tags, but about deep, warm caring that says, "If you have something to laugh about or cry about, bring it here. You belong here. We know your name!"

What would it take to make your church a place where people come because they know they will be recognized and warmly accepted—where they can be blessed?

The cup of blessing which we bless, is it not the communion of the blood of Christ? The bread which we break, is it not the communion of the body of Christ? For we, though many, are one bread and one body; for we all partake of that one bread. —1 COR. 10:16–17

Communion is a tremendous way for us to face the greatest blessing of all, God's priceless sacrifice of His Son for our sins. Whether your church calls this celebration the Eucharist or the Lord's Supper, whether you celebrate it daily or quarterly, this special event offers a wonderful opportunity for the church family to draw together in thanksgiving.

In preparation for Communion, why not honor the Lord by taking the time to strengthen the bonds of love among the congregation? If someone in the congregation has dishonored someone else, he or she can be encouraged to go to that person and ask forgiveness and set things right. A congregation blesses God when it approaches the Communion table in a spirit of unity and love.

The next time you participate in Communion, do so in a spirit of blessing.

Greet one another with a holy kiss. The churches of
Christ greet you.
—ROM. 16:16

Here's a checklist to help you assess your success in giving the blessing at your church—and to motivate you to more deliberately bless others.

1. Do you take the time to greet other church members warmly?
2. Do you regularly share a friendly hug or hearty handshake?
3. Do you pray for members of the congregation?
4. Do you let the pastor and other leaders know when they have done a good job?
5. Do you encourage the younger members?
6. Do you fellowship (socialize) with any members outside of church?
7. Do you bring others to your church?
8. Do you share what you are learning in Sunday school/church with others?
9. Does someone in the congregation make you feel important?
10. Is there someone whom you feel could benefit from your blessing?*

A church's blessing is only as strong as each member's commitment.

*Prepared for use in the Family Emphasis Series at the Metropolitan church of God, Detroit, Michigan. Contributed by Stella R. Calloway.

> *Meditate on these things. . . . that your progress*
> *may be evident to all.*
> —1 TIM. 4:15

Meditate on these everyday blessings parents have given to children:

1. When I started wearing makeup, my mother never made fun of how much time I spent in front of the mirror.
2. Even though I was very overweight in high school, my parents still made me feel attractive.
3. Mom took a part-time job to help me earn enough money to go to a Christian summer camp.
4. My parents paid for me to take several vocational tests when I was struggling to find out what I wanted to do for a living.
5. My father would reward me for yard work well done by taking me to Dairy Queen®, where we would both get a sundae.
6. My father let me share his failures as well as his successes.
7. My father went with me to six different used car dealers to help me find my first car.
8. My parents made sure each of us children met their friends when they came to our house.

How can the church support parents who are trying to bless their children? Husbands and wives trying to bless their mates? Friends blessing friends?

*There shall be showers of blessing. . . . Thus they
shall know that I, the LORD their God, am with
them.*
                                    —EZEK. 34:26,30

We can extend the blessing to others inside and outside the church in so many creative ways—and most of
them begin with opening our eyes to another's needs.

One woman told us that in her church, after reading
about the blessing, "Two sensitive ladies noticed a
twenty-one-year-old girl who always enjoyed others'
bridal and baby showers, but would never experience
them herself. Due to mental and physical disabilities,
she would remain single and at home." They decided
to give her a blessing party and have each guest share
specially how God had used her life to minister to
them. That time together was probably the most wor-
shipful party those ladies had ever attended.

*Use your quiet time this morning to list five people you know from
church who may be blessing-hungry. (If you don't know anyone well
enough to make a list, that may be a signal that it's time to reach
out!) Pray about specific ways you can help fill the blessing void in
these people's lives.*

> *And as His custom was, He went into the*
> *synagogue on the Sabbath.*
> —LUKE 4:16

Pastor and author James Hewett suggests a simple concept that can help you make the blessing a more integral part of your church and personal life. He suggests we put the power of habit to work by setting up *structures* to help us do what we want to do. "By structures I mean *habitual patterns* or methods planned ahead of time and carried out regularly. Structures are like miniature, built-in, repeatable plans.... When you have a structure, you don't have to re-invent the wheel."* A structure could be anything from going to church on Sundays to keeping a grocery list on the refrigerator. However, it is set up ahead of time so it can proceed without much extra thought or effort; we just do it because it is our custom.

How can you structure a blessing? A church could set aside a regular part of the worship service for blessing or an annual blessings retreat. A family could tie blessings to bedtime or another daily ritual. The particulars don't matter, as long as the chosen structure helps weave blessings into everyday life.

What are some practical ways you can structure the blessing into your personal and church lives?

*James Hewett, *How to Live Confidently in a Hostile World* (Dallas: Word, 1989).

Take heed that you do not despise one of these little ones, for I say to you that in heaven their angels always see the face of My Father who is in heaven. For the Son of Man has come to save that which was lost.

—MATT. 18:10–11

The church can fill a vital role in blessing children whose home situations have left them with a "blessing deficit." Our church has found two programs to be especially successful in blessing children from single-parent homes.

The first is a "Big Brother/Big Sister" program designed to provide for the needs of boys and girls who are missing elements of the blessing from a parent. By matching an adult male with a young boy and an adult female with a young girl, gaping holes caused by a missing parental blessing can be filled.

The second program is "Adopt a Grandparent." This program matches a single-parent child (or a child whose grandparents live far away) with a member of the senior department. Each can become a source of blessing to the other. As one six-year-old commented, "Grandparents are the only adults who have time to listen."

What are some other ways the church can reach out to meet a child's blessing deficit? How can you get involved in such a ministry?

You, O God, provided from Your goodness for the poor.
—PS. 68:10

Many churches are involved in outreach programs that help the needy in their communities. Perhaps your church runs a soup kitchen, a clothes closet, a thrift shop, or a day-care center. Keeping the elements of the blessing in mind can help transform these vital helping ministries into instruments of transformation.

We don't mean formal, pronounced words of blessing. But taking the time to touch a hand and speak words of appreciation ("I always enjoy your sense of humor!") and hope ("I really do think we can help you turn things around!") can turn a helping hand into a touch of grace. And of course, the active commitment of being there speaks a powerful blessing to someone in need.

You have the opportunity not only to help the poor, but to bless them!

*Remember those who rule over you, who have
spoken the word of God to you.*   —HEB. 13:7

Most lay people in the church rely on the professional ministers among them for a source of blessing. That's not inappropriate. The "shepherd" does have the joyful responsibility of blessing the "sheep" and leading them in the direction of the blessing.

But the minister was never meant to be the only "blesser" in a congregation. And ministers need blessings too! In fact, the very nature of the job—always on call, always running the risk of someone's displeasure, and often being underpaid—may make some ministers especially hungry for words of blessing.

As you consider ways to make your church a place of blessing, don't forget the one who leads you. Reach out with a friendly touch, words of appreciation and hope, and the promise of faithful commitment.

During your quiet time today, pray for the ministers in your church. Ask God to bless them and to show you ways to give them the elements of the blessing.

> *Then they also brought infants to Him that He*
> *might touch them.*
> —LUKE 18:15

One way to weave the blessing into a congregation's life is to plan a special blessing service. One woman described an especially meaningful "Blessing of the Children" held in her church:

The people came to the front by families for Communion. At this time, those desiring that their children be blessed had been instructed to move to the sides, where lines formed in front of the elders giving the blessing. Everyone came—even the teens. It took the entire morning to work through the congregation, but many said it was the most beautiful service of worship in their lives. We knew we were in the presence of the Lord! Surely what we were witnessing was akin to the events of Jesus' day, where people with babies in arms stood waiting patiently for their turn. I'd often wondered how the little ones in those long-ago throngs could wait patiently. But now I realized that in the presence of Jesus, their spirits were quieted too.

What can you do to see the blessing become part of your church's worship?

*From what the LORD has blessed you with, you
shall give to him.*
                                    —DEUT. 15:14

Oh, no, not another stewardship campaign!"

Many of us—clergy and laity alike—groan when
church budget time rolls around. We're more comfortable talking about spiritual things—not line items and
expenses. And nobody likes to feel someone else has
a hand in his or her pocket.

But budgets are important to "blessing manage-
ment" at home and church. After all, money and material possessions are just another form of blessing—a
gift we receive and can pass on to others. And the attitudes that inform our giving and receiving of other
kinds of blessings should inform the way we manage
our financial blessings. We receive in gratitude. And
we give in abundance, trusting that our heavenly Father has plenty more blessings to give us.

*Financial blessings, like other kinds of blessings, do the most good
when passed on instead of hoarded.*

*And there you shall eat before the LORD your God,
and you shall rejoice in all to which you have put
your hand, you and your households, in which the
LORD your God has blessed you.* —DEUT. 12:7

You say it's been too long since your last church potluck dinner? Why not have a special "blessings potluck"? For a fun variation on the traditional potluck,
ask each family to bring a dish that says something
about their ethnic or geographic roots—Swedish meat-
balls, French pastry, whatever. Sharing a meal like this
is a great way to get to know each other better.*

As an admission ticket to the dinner, each adult
should bring a Bible verse that has blessed his or her
life. At some point in the evening, share these verses
with the entire group or around the tables. After that,
the program is up to you. Singing hymns, sharing word
pictures, or even honoring individual members for
their contributions are great ways to celebrate and
give blessings. In some churches, a foot-washing service could be a way to bow the knee to a brother or
sister in Christ. Close the ceremony of blessing by
holding hands and singing a closing chorus or benedic-
tion.

---

*An evening of TV can't hold a candle to an evening of gathering as
a church family to bless each other and thank God for His blessings.*

* This suggestion is based on a creative church family evening in the excellent
book by Marlene D. LeFever, *Creative Hospitality* (Wheaton, IL: Tyndale
House Publishers, 1980), p. 26.

*For the LORD has blessed His people; and what is
left is this great abundance.*   —2 CHRON. 31:10

Counting your blessings" can be a particularly fulfilling exercise when done as a congregation. One church
did this by setting up a large, blank poster during a
dinner. Each table was equipped with pencils, paper,
and straight pins. After a short message on God's faithfulness in blessing the congregation over the years, the
pastor asked each person to write down one way God
had blessed him or her during the previous year.
Those who wanted could come up to the front, share
their blessings, and pin their papers on the blank
poster. By the end of the evening, dozens of testimo-
nies filled that poster, and the room glowed with joy
and gratitude.

A fun variation of such an exercise could be held
during the Christmas season. Set up a "Blessings Tree"
and let church members fill it with paper ornaments
listing blessings.

*Why not set up a time with a small group of Christian friends or a
section of your church family to do a group "blessings count" and
thank God together?*

For I desire mercy and not sacrifice,
and the knowledge of God more than burnt offerings.
—HOS. 6:6

Thanksgiving is coming soon—the traditional time of formal prayers and abundant feasting. (For some families, it's also a time of "burnt offerings"!) But this verse reminds us that God is more interested in our inner attitudes than any outward or formal religious show. We thank Him best by becoming more sensitive to others' needs and more deeply committed to blessing others.

With this in mind, why not concentrate on making this Thanksgiving a festival of mercy? If tensions exist in your family circle, seek reconciliation. Make apologies. Ask forgiveness. Pray together. And then, reach out! If you know anyone who is away from home, share the blessings of friendship in your home. And for a special blessing, volunteer as a family to serve in a nearby homeless mission (and plan to go back to help again later). In one way or another, all these blessings will return to you, and your gratitude will be doubled.

Make this Thanksgiving a celebration of mercy and blessing.

*Now may the God of peace who brought up our
Lord Jesus from the dead . . . make you complete
in every good work to do His will, working in you
what is well pleasing in His sight.*

—HEB. 13:20–21

We have gradually painted a picture of how the blessing can enrich our lives. We have used broad strokes to illustrate how the blessing was viewed down through the centuries. We have also used the fine strokes of the literal meaning of the word *blessing* to bring out the nuances of this concept. Five predominant patterns run through the painting, each an important element of the blessing. Together they give the viewer a sense of structure and balance. Stories of people, past and present, have brought color and depth to the picture. Some of these colors are dark and stir our compassion. Yet we have also tried to paint brilliant colors of joy, happiness, and security from the lives of those who have received the blessing.

However, before we lay down our brush and leave this "blessing portrait," we must paint one final corner—which is a key to capturing our picture's total scope. It portrays children returning the blessing to their parents.

Whether your parents are living or dead, you can make a full circle by blessing them.

*Cursed is the one who treats his father or his
mother with contempt.*
—DEUT. 27:16

Not all parents, of course, are easy to bless—or even worthy of the blessing. That was certainly the case with Helen, the woman whose father had abused her so cruelly before she found a safe haven in God's spiritual family, the church. Not surprisingly, she never wanted to see her father again.

But after she had been a Christian for awhile, Helen noted that certain areas of her spiritual life were lagging. She had grown much, but she still had a nasty temper and a tendency to criticize others. At first, Helen thought these problems were due to a lack of faith. But one day she realized the real problem was her ongoing bitterness toward her father. She had still not opened her relationship with him to God's leadership, healing, and love. Unless she dealt with the stranglehold he still held on her life, she would continue to struggle in her spiritual life and personal relationships. She realized her need to bless her father anyway—for her own sake.

Blessing our parents is not optional—even when they don't deserve it. Our own spiritual and emotional health depends on our returning the blessing full circle.

I have set before you life and death, blessing and cursing; therefore choose life, that both you and your descendants may live. —DEUT. 30:19

Yesterday we looked again at Helen, who realized her own spiritual life depended on her choosing to bless the father who had abused her. After much struggle and prayer—and many sessions with her pastor—Helen knocked on the door of a man she hadn't seen for fifteen years. She was surprised to find her father looking so old and tired. And after she poured out her heart—telling about becoming a Christian, admitting her anger and hatred, asking his forgiveness—she was astounded to see tears in his eyes. For the first time, he faced the burning conviction of his wrongs against his daughter. He lamented the pain he had caused her and begged for her forgiveness. Helen put her arms around her father and spoke the words she never thought she could say: "I love you, Daddy."

When Helen came to know Christ, He had freed her from sin and unlocked the shackles that chained her to the past. By having the courage to honor and bless her father, Helen removed the shackles Christ had unlocked. She walked away from her father's house free to live in the present.

How would this story be different if Helen's father had not been repentant? How would Helen have dealt with her need to forgive?

Make a joyful shout to the LORD, all you lands! . . .
Be thankful to Him, and bless His name.
—PS. 100:1, 4

Here's a blessing from Psalm 100 to pronounce over your Thanksgiving table and share with one another:

Today, dear Lord, we come before You with a joyful shout! May we always serve You with gladness and come before Your presence with singing. We know that You are God. You have made us, and not we ourselves. We are Your people and the sheep of Your pasture. That is why we will enter into Your gates with thanksgiving and into Your courts with praise. We thank You, and we bless Your name. For You are good. Your mercy is everlasting. And Your truth endures to all generations.

In your quiet time today, meditate on who God is and the reason you have to thank Him enthusiastically. Praise Him!

Honor your father and mother.
—EPH. 6:2

Do only those like Helen, who have such a hurtful past, need to bless their parents? Certainly not. The Scriptures direct *every* child to give the blessing to his or her parents. In the book of Ephesians, Paul goes into detail about healthy family relationships, and his instructions to children reiterate one of the Ten Commandments: "Honor your father and mother."

What does it mean to honor your parents? In Hebrew, the word for "honor" is *kabed,* which literally means, "to be heavy, weighty, to honor."* We still use that meaning today. When the President of the United States or some other important person speaks, people often say that his words "carry a lot of weight." When Paul tells us to honor our parents, he tells us that they are worthy of high value and respect.

Honoring our parents mean to "weigh them heavy" in our lives.
*Hebrew Lexicon, p. 457.

*In you they have made light of father and
mother. . . . Can your heart endure, or can your
hands remain strong, in the days when I shall deal
with you?*
—EZEK. 22:7, 14

Yesterday we learned that the Hebrew word for "honor" literally means "to be heavy"—so honoring someone means to let them "carry weight" in our lives. The opposite is true as well. As we discovered earlier, the Hebrew word for "curse" means "to make light of."* And today, if we dishonor a person, we would say, "Their words carry little weight." The contrast is striking!

Some people treat their parents as if they are dust on a table. Dust weighs almost nothing and can be swept away with a brush of the hand. Dust is a nuisance and an eyesore that clouds the real beauty of the table. Scripture tells us that such an attitude should not be a part of the way any child views his or her parents. If we fail to honor our parents, we not only dishonor God, but we also drain ourselves of life.

*What circumstances in your life might cause you to "make light of"
your parents instead of honoring them?*

*Ibid., p. 866.

*"Honor your father and mother," which is the first
commandment with promise.*
—EPH. 6:2

Children love it when their parents promise them
good things—an ice cream cone, a trip to the zoo, a
story. And wise parents often use such promises to
teach their children behaviors and character traits that
will bring them happiness. God uses promises to teach
His children, too. In fact, the apostle Paul reminds us
that "honor your father and your mother" is the first of
the Ten Commandments to have a promise attached.

However, we must remember two things about
God's promises. First, God always keeps his promises.
But second, as we saw earlier, God's promises are often conditional. They may depend on our filling certain conditions—in this case, honoring our parents. It's
our choice. We can choose to dishonor our parents, but
if we do, we will live apart from God's promise. And
what exactly does God promise to those who honor
their parents? We will explore some specific benefits
in the next few days.

*What specific benefits can you see accruing from a decision to honor
our parents whether or not they deserve the honor?*

> *"Honor your father and mother," which is the first*
> *commandment with promise: "that it may be well*
> *with you."*
> —EPH. 6:2–3

Children thrive on their parents' approval. Anyone who has sat in a playground listening to children scream, "Daddy, look at me! Mom, look!" realizes children constantly perform for their parents. Anyone who has seen a small child labor over a drawing and then present it proudly to Mom or Dad understands children live to hear the significant people in their lives say, "Wow, you did great!"

That kind of loving approval is at the heart of the first promise Paul attached to honoring our parents. In New Testament Greek, this entire phrase is captured in the tiny word, *eu*, which means "well." In ancient Greece, this word was used to salute someone with the words, "Well done! Excellent!"* The first part of the promise God extends to those who honor their parents is, "If you do this, I will be pleased and say, 'Well done!'"

What kind of motivation does the promise of pleasing God provide for you personally? In what ways can you feel His pleasure and approval? What difference do they make in your life?

*Arndt and Gingrich, *Greek-English Lexicon*, p. 317.

"Hypocrites! Well did Isaiah prophesy about you, saying:

> *'These people draw near to Me with their mouth,*
> *and honor Me with their lips,*
> *but their heart is far from Me.'"*

—MATT. 15:7–8

For God's people, pleasing Him has always included treating parents well. In Leviticus 19:3, for example, Moses commanded the people, "Every one of you shall revere his mother and his father, and keep My Sabbaths." Linked with the importance of setting aside a special Sabbath day each week to honor God is the command to consistently honor your parents.

Jesus also felt our actions toward our parents reflect our heart toward God. He aimed His acid words in today's scripture directly at the Pharisees and Scribes who used their religious traditions to avoid supporting their parents. For Jesus, doing what was wrong by dishonoring parents could never be linked with what was right in God's eyes. Anyone who urges us to dishonor our parents—for whatever reason—speaks words of hypocrisy and falsehood. We will only hear a "well done" from our heavenly Father when we choose to honor our parents.

What kind of arguments do you hear from those who urge you not to honor your parents? Which of these arguments are most persuasive? How do you think Jesus would answer them?

> *"Honor your father and mother," which is the first*
> *commandment with promise: "that it may be well*
> *with you and you may live long on the earth."*
> —EPH. 6:2–3

God's second promise for those who honor their parents is that they will actually receive long life. How can this be? Ask many physicians, counselors, or pastors. They have seen the shattered lives of those who dishonor their parents and are drained of strength as a result. Physicians and researchers are finding that a close link exists between what we think and how our bodies react. Positive attitudes have been linked with positive physiological changes, while negative attitudes can open the door for illness or disease.*

It's not a cut-and-dried connection, of course. This scripture does not guarantee that honoring your parents will automatically make you immune to cancer or safe from drunken drivers. (Many other factors come into play, including a fallen creation and the sins of other people.) But this scripture does present the principle that our health and well-being depend on positive attitudes toward those who brought us into the world.

Our general health and physical well-being are directly linked to our decision to honor our parents.

*Gerald C. Davison and John M. Neale, *Abnormal Psychology* (New York: John Wiley & Sons, 1978), p. 135ff.

When I kept silent about my sin, my body wasted away through my groaning all day long.
For day and night, Thy hand was heavy upon me; my vitality was drained away as with the fever heat of summer.

—PS. 32:3–4 NASB

Scripture supports the strong connection between our inner attitudes and our physical health. In Proverbs 17:22, for example, we read, "A merry heart does good, like medicine, / But a broken spirit dries the bones." Today's Scripture outlines the ongoing misery of remaining in bondage to bitterness.

When you decide to honor your parents and place high value on them, God says such actions will increase your life on the earth and make it worth living. But if you decide to clutch bitterness or resentment (attitudes of dishonor), you not only run the risk of shortening your life; you drain your energy so that you cannot enjoy your life.

Pray for the insight to know whether you have dishonored your parents through your actions or attitudes. Pray for the courage and strength to begin the process of correcting this. Rest in the knowledge that God never commands you to do the impossible!

But we are bound to give thanks to God always for you.
—2 THESS. 2:13

Here are more everyday blessings we have heard for children of all ages:

1. My parents quit using a nickname that hurt me.
2. My mom used to rub my legs after cheerleader practice.
3. My father would always point out my good table manners to others.
4. My mother would see that I had the necessary tools to complete a project (crayons, ruler).
5. My father would put a special note on our pillows when he had to leave town on business.
6. My parents involved the whole family in planning vacations.
7. My father took me and my sisters on special dates for our sixteenth birthdays.
8. My folks would always go to my piano recitals and act interested.
9. My father would let me practice pitching to him when he got home from work.

As you move from the Thanksgiving season into the Christmas season, reflect on the blessings your own parents have given you and on the blessings you want to pass on.

Prepare the way of the LORD;
make straight in the desert
a highway for our God.
—ISA. 40:3

Christmas is coming! Every store is tinsel-draped; every street corner hung with lights. Every day the newspaper ominously announces how many shopping days we have left.

In the church, these weeks before Christmas are traditionally a time of preparation, too. But instead of a frenzy of shopping and wrapping, we are called to prepare our souls for the Lord's coming. That is what the word *Advent* means. Traditionally, this before-Christmas time is to be a season of quiet anticipation, of repentance, of forgiveness, and reconciliation.

It's not easy to concentrate on such inward things with all the bustle going on. Sometimes it may sound like one more hard job on top of too many overwhelming tasks. But surely, making peace with one another and learning to bless each other is one of the best ways to "make straight in the desert a highway for our God."

Make time for repentance and forgiveness during your hectic holidays, so the blessing of Christmas may fill your heart.

> *There is a kind of man who curses his father,*
> *and does not bless his mother.*
> *There is a kind who is pure in his own eyes,*
> *yet is not washed from his filthiness.*
> *There is a kind—oh how lofty are his eyes!*
> *and his eyelids are raised in arrogance.*
> *There is a kind of man whose teeth are like swords,*
> *and his jaw teeth like knives.*
> —PROV. 30:11–14 NASB

The Bible clearly indicates that we need to honor our parents for our own good. Yet, how do we do this? The whole book of Proverbs gives us a hint: we honor our parents by acting as wise people, not as fools. Many of the Proverbs illustrate different kinds of "fools" who do not apply God's principles for right living. One vivid description is found in today's scripture. Look at this worthless, treacherous man. Then see what heads the list of his characteristics.

The man pictured above brings pain to those inside and outside the home not only by cursing his parents, but also for failing to bless them! That, of course, brings us back to giving our parents the blessing.

In providing the blessing to your parents, you truly honor them, do what is right in God's eyes, and even prolong your life.

> *The angel said to her, "Rejoice, highly favored one,*
> *the Lord is with you; blessed are you among*
> *women!" . . . Mary said, . . . "Let it be to me*
> *according to your word."*
>   —LUKE 1:28,38

What is more exciting about this wonderful pre-Christmas passage—the angel's exciting message of blessing or Mary's whole-hearted acceptance?

We all long for a blessing, but many of us find it hard to accept the blessings we are given. For a number of reasons—family upbringing, our own sense of shame, guilt over not blessing others—we squirm when someone reaches to us with words of high value, special future, and active commitment. We want to mumble something like "Aw, shucks," instead of "Let it be to me according to your word."

But one thing that has emerged from this year of study and prayer is that it's hard to bless others when we don't feel blessed. Learning to open our hearts to the blessings we're given is a crucial part of learning to give the blessing.

Lord, teach me to open up and accept the blessings you send my way.

> *Honor your father and your mother, as the LORD*
> *your God has commanded you, that your days may*
> *be long, and that it may be well with you in the*
> *land which the Lord your God is giving you.*
> —DEUT. 5:16

We have talked about the five elements of the blessing. We have seen these elements applied to children, spouses, friends, and the church family. Yet these elements can also provide a blessing for our parents. In the next week, we will examine how we can work the five elements of the blessing into our parental relationship. We will consider emotional barriers that hinder us from blessing the ones who raised us.

Perhaps your parents are dead, suffering from senile dementia, or inaccessible. This doesn't mean you don't need to honor them (remember, the honoring is for your sake, too), but you will obviously have difficulty applying some of the suggestions for giving the elements of blessing. Even if this is true, we urge you to prayerfully consider your ongoing attitudes toward your parents, as well as your actions toward others of their generation. Later, we will look at strategies for blessing your parents or their memories.

To prepare for the next meditations, prayerfully consider some effective ways of giving the blessing to your parents or other older people.

Now also when I am old and grayheaded . . .
do not forsake me.   —PS. 71:18

Meaningful touch is the first element of the blessing you give to anyone. Your parents are no exception. Even if they have struggled with hugging and touching when you were young, as they grow older they need the reassurance that comes from being touched.

This element of the blessing is especially important in a culture that worships youth and devalues older persons—especially women. In our culture, being "touchable" is usually equated with being young, active, unwrinkled. But the need for respectful touch has no age boundaries. The need for meaningful touch doesn't leave because we become older. So don't forget to make a hug or a pat on the back part of the blessing you give your parents and any older person. (This is especially important for seniors who live alone.)

What barriers of culture or background hold you back from touching your parents? What are some practical ways you can make touch a bigger part of your relationship?

*And may he be to you a restorer of life and a
nourisher of your old age.*
—RUTH 4:15

Isn't it interesting that Mother's Day is the busiest day of the year for interstate phone calls! For many mothers, those calls will constitute the only encouraging words they hear from their children until the next year. Unfortunately, many fathers hear fewer spoken words of praise.

The transition from being dependent on our parents and being responsible for our relationship with them is sometimes tricky. In a sense, we are always our parents' children, dependent on them for our blessing. Part of growing up, however, is learning to see our parents as humans with needs of their own—including the need for *a spoken message* of blessing. That's why you need to be consistently in contact with your parents. They need to hear your voice and its restoring words of blessing.

Are you comfortable with speaking (or writing) words of blessing to your parents? Are you consistent in this? If not, why not? Make this element of blessing for your parents a matter of ongoing prayer.

A wise son makes a father glad,
But a foolish man despises his mother.
—PROV. 15:20

Parents too often remember the past with guilt. Memories that stand out to them are not the many positive things they did, but the times they spoke in anger or accidentally hurt their children. By blessing your parents with words that *attach high value* to them, you can tremendously encourage their lives. You do not need to pretend a wrong was never committed. But you can face the issue and state your forgiveness. You can also praise them for the things they did right.

Obviously, this element of the blessing will be hardest for people with painful childhood memories. Much strength is needed to attach high value to a person who evidently didn't value you very much. In fact, such an act of forgiveness and blessing is probably impossible from a human standpoint; we can only do it in God's strength.

As we become secure in God's blessing, we must value our parents—for the good they have done, for the act of giving us life, and also because we recognize that they, too, are valued by our heavenly Father.

> *They shall still bear fruit . . .*
> *They shall be fresh and flourishing.*
> —PS. 92:14

Parents need words that picture a *special future* for them. In fact, parents who dwell on the past may do so because they do not feel a sense of a future in their lives. No matter what your parents' ages, you can bless them by pointing out useful and beneficial aspects of their lives—even if those qualities are different from when they were younger. You can also encourage them that their future with their heavenly Father and spiritual family does not end with this life.

To do this, you may need to examine your own attitudes about aging and the meaning of life. Have you unconsciously bought our cultural assumptions that life goes downhill after forty—or even after thirty? Do you value the vitality of youth over the wisdom of age—or assume there is no vitality in age? What are your own feelings about death and eternal life?

Don't accept the common myths that life is over when youth is gone. Study Scripture to challenge these lies. Be alert to news articles about active seniors who make a valuable contribution. Keep these realities in your own mind and use them to encourage your parents.

My son, hear the instruction of your father,
And do not forsake the law of your mother;
—PROV. 1:8

Assuring your parents of their important place in the family as the years go by is helpful. In some homes with older parents, the grown children take over the finances and major decisions and ignore the older parent's input. Nothing is wrong with helping your parents, but make sure you still honor them in the process. By continuing to ask for their words of wisdom, you provide them with a picture of a special future—and can benefit from the advice!

You can also encourage a special future for your parents by letting them be part of your future—especially the future wrapped up in your children. Providing the time for grandparents and grandchildren to interact can provide your parents with a special future.

If you let your parents know how they can be and have been an integral force in your family, you honor them.

December 10 – ONGOING COMMITMENT

You say, "Whoever says to his father or mother,
'Whatever profit you might have received from me
is a gift to God'—then he need not honor his father
or mother." Thus you have made the commandment
of God of no effect by your tradition. Hypocrites!
—MATT. 15:5–7

Of all the ways you can honor your parents, the genuine commitment to walk with them through each step in life is particularly important. This commitment is not only an element of blessing; it is a God-ordained duty. In Matthew 15, Jesus saved His most scathing words for Pharisees who used religious tradition as an excuse for abandoning this long-term commitment.

Even though the popular picture of inevitable decline and decay is a dangerous stereotype, the second half of life still presents rigorous challenges. If they haven't already, your parents will cope with physical changes, trying to steer through retirement and perhaps the rigors of a fixed income, watching as friends and family—and perhaps a mate—die, and coming to terms with their own approaching death. Your active commitment to stand beside them as they face these challenges can be an enormous blessing. Particularly when one parent dies, the other will need an extra measure of your ongoing love and commitment.

We bless our parents especially effectively when we make it clear that we are with them all the way.

> *I know your works, love, service, faith, and your patience; and as for your works, the last are more than the first.*
>
> —REV. 2:19

These words, spoken by the risen Christ to the church of Thyatira, can give comfort to those struggling to bless their parents under difficult circumstances such as these:

Those whose parents remain cantankerous, abusive, and stubborn.

Those whose spouse and parents don't get along and thus feel pulled in half.

Those members of the "sandwich generation" who juggle the care of children with the needs of older parents—often holding down jobs as well.

Those who agonize over hard decisions: "Can Dad still live alone?" "Can we afford nursing care?" "Should I quit my job to help Mom?" "Should we choose a 'no code' if something goes wrong?"

Those caring for a parent who no longer recognizes them.

To all of you who are struggling to be faithful, remember: the Lord knows your works—and blesses your efforts. On your difficult days, draw on His strength and try to live in the sunshine of His love.

If you do not struggle with these kinds of issues, be aware of the pain of those who do. You can bless them with your prayers and offers of practical help.

Whoever curses his father or his mother, His lamp will be put out in deep darkness. —PROV. 20:20

We know the idea of blessing your parents may be especially hard for you to accept. You may still be saying, "Bless *my* parents? How can you say that? You just don't know them . . ." We don't deny for a moment that some parents, from a human perspective, are almost impossible to bless. We've heard their stories in many counseling sessions. But as much as we may long for an exception clause, we can't mistake the clear command of Scripture that we honor our mother and father—and we can't ignore the "deep darkness" ongoing bitterness brings.

But let's be clear. Deciding to honor our parents does not mean we let an alcoholic father drive our children across the city. It doesn't mean calling our verbally abusive mother every day when each call is an invitation for further attack. It does mean making a decision to attach value to our parents, to "weigh them heavy" despite their shortcomings, and to keep the door open to forgiveness and reconciliation.

Honoring your parents doesn't mean letting them abuse you. Pray for wisdom and grace to know the difference.

Take heed to yourselves. If your brother sins against you, rebuke him; and if he repents, forgive him.
—LUKE 17:3

No matter whom you want to bless, or whether your past has been basically happy or a constant torment, the act of blessing another person will inevitably involve forgiveness. If the blessing is genuine, we must move beyond past hurts and commit ourselves anew to a positive future.

How can we "forgive and forget" when someone has hurt us deeply? Actually, forgetting is not the issue. Trying to forget can even be harmful if it means minimizing our pain or making excuses for those who have hurt us. Until we can acknowledge that someone we cared about has "done us wrong," we cannot begin the process of forgiving him or her.

Even Jesus told us to "rebuke" first, then forgive. The basic question of forgiveness is not pretending there was no injury, but facing the pain and choosing to forgive it.

> *Judge not, and you shall not be judged. Condemn not, and you shall not be condemned. Forgive, and you will be forgiven.*
>
> —LUKE 6:37

If forgiveness is not forgetting, what is it?

When we forgive someone, we make a choice of the will to leave judging and condemning to God. We depend on Him to help us continue in the way we have chosen, the way He commands—the way of forgiveness.

When we forgive, we say in essence: "I have been hurt. My pain is real, and I have the right to be resentful. Yet I know that my heavenly Father has forgiven me for my sins and wants me to forgive as well. And I recognize that holding on to my pain hurts me more than it could ever hurt the other person. For these reasons, and relying on God's help, I give up my right to condemn the people who have hurt me."

Is the need for forgiveness an issue in your ability to give someone a blessing?

And if he sins against you seven times in a day, and seven times in a day returns to you, saying, "I repent," you shall forgive him.
—LUKE 17:4

Saying "I forgive you" doesn't magically free you of resentment! You can make the choice to forgive and still feel angry . . . and feel guilty because you haven't "really forgiven"! How can you begin to bless others under these circumstances? Today's scripture hints at an insight that Dr. Archibald Hart elaborates:

Forgiveness is both an act and a *process.* It is an act of your will in which you choose to surrender your right to hurt those who have hurt you, and it is a continual process of choosing forgiveness until you finally feel forgiveness. . . . Every time the hurt arises—and it will—you remind yourself, 'I have already forgiven this hurt.' And then you deliberately behave as if you have already forgiven. . . . [This] *begins* the process of spiritual healing. . . . Psychologically, you are reinforcing the right attitude.*

Providing elements of the blessing is an important part of behaving "as if you have already forgiven." In that sense, blessing the people you want to forgive reinforces your experience of forgiveness!

*Archibald D. Hart, *Healing Adult Children of Divorce* (Ann Arbor: Servant Publications, 1991), p. 126.

We speak, not as pleasing men, but God who tests our hearts.
—1 THESS. 2:4

Helen's story of honoring an abusive father has a happy ending. But not every act of forgiveness results in reconciliation. Not every overture of blessing will be returned. You may reach out in love and forgiveness, only to receive a slap on the face.

That is why you must remember that blessing someone and forgiving him or her is a choice *you* make. You accept the reality that forgiveness is something God commands, something you do in response to His love, something you must do to be a whole, loving, healthy person.

It is wise, to forgive and bless people with *no* expectations about their responses. Don't expect them to admit guilt or even to agree about what has happened. Don't wait for response or applause before continuing the act of blessing. Instead, do it to please your heavenly Father, who knows your heart and wants you to be blessed.

A positive response from the person you are forgiving is a wonderful gift . . . but it's really beside the point. The real point is pleasing God.

When I remember these things, I pour out my soul within me.
—PS. 42:4

Practically speaking, how do you bless a parent who has died? You must deal with your memory of that person, which may be as vivid as their actual presence. If you loved your parents deeply but never told them so, you can bless them by honoring their memory. If you struggle with a painful past, you can bless them by coming to terms with that pain.

The first step in coming to terms with the memory of your parents is to share your feelings and concern with the Lord. You may also want to talk to a trusted friend, your pastor, or a Christian counselor. Then, why not write a letter—or make a cassette tape—to share what you would like to say to your absent parent. If it helps, symbolically "mail" the letter by burning it or setting it adrift in a stream. Then, commit yourself to an ongoing process of honoring your parents in memory.

Being free to be a person of blessing requires dealing honestly with the past. Even if you have only the memory of your parents, you can still honor them and make things right between the Lord and your memory of them.

> *Let the heavens rejoice, and let the earth be glad;*
> *Let the sea roar, and all its fullness;*
> *Let the field be joyful, and all that is in it.*
> *Then all the trees of the woods will rejoice before*
>   *the LORD.*
> *For He is coming. . . .*
>   —PS. 96:11–13

Joy to the world!" These days, you hear it in every elevator and on every radio station. And it's one of our favorite hymns. It portrays the same jubilant excitement as this Psalm. The Lord is coming. The Lord is come!

The fourth element of the blessing, remember, is picturing a special future. Again and again in Scripture, the Lord blesses us by picturing in vivid terms the wonderful future in store for those who love Him. Yes, pain will occur during the time between "The Lord is come"—Christ's life, death, and resurrection—and "The Lord is coming"—His promise to return. But even in the midst of suffering, what a blessing of anticipation we are given.

Lord, thank You for the blessing of anticipating You. "Even so, come, Lord Jesus" (Rev. 22:20).

Let your father and your mother be glad, And let her who bore you rejoice. —PROV. 23:25

Cindy and I (John) have been to some very creative parties over the years. From "Regressive Dinners" to "Roaring Twenties" nights, we thought we had seen them all. Then an invitation came that really caught our attention. We were asked to attend a surprise "This Is Your Life" party for an older couple in our church. The party had been planned by the children to honor their parents for years of loving care and sacrifice. By the time the evening was finished, no eyes were dry! As we left this older couple's house, we could see their hearts were bursting with pride, appreciation, and love. That evening was worth far more to them than any gift their children could have ever purchased.

Has it been too long since you honored your parents with words of blessing? You only need an active commitment to give back to them what God has already richly given you.

You do not know what will happen tomorrow.
—JAMES 4:14

Consider honoring your parents with an evening of blessing. This could be a perfect opportunity to give back words of love and acceptance you have received.

Don't assume "my parents would never let us do something like that for them!" True, many parents who are used to giving the elements of the blessing may not be as used to receiving them. However, time and again embarrassed or uncomfortable parents have still treasured their times of blessing for the rest of their lives.

Don't avoid an evening of blessing because one parent has died or because your parents have divorced. Be sensitive, but you can still honor the absent parent and provide needed words of love and encouragement to the remaining parent. (If your parents are divorced, you may want to have a separate time of blessing for each one.)

You really don't know what tomorrow will bring. So don't wait until it's too late to share words of blessing with your parents. Through a special evening or some other act of honor, make sure they receive a blessing from you.

*A time to weep,
and a time to laugh.*
—ECCL. 3:4

What would it take to organize a special evening for your parents? If you have brothers and sisters, gather all of them for your special time of blessing. (If someone absolutely can't come, get him or her to send an audio or video tape of some words of blessing. Consider recording the entire evening so the parent will have a permanent memory.)

What should you do during your evening of blessing? A special dinner (with firm orders *not* to help clean up) is a great way to start. Sharing photos, slides, or home movies can help everyone remember fun family times, but prepare special words of blessing, too. For instance, each child can share five positive character traits your parents built into his or her life. Present your parents with a homemade gift or a special portrait of the children. Close the evening with a time of prayer, with everyone gathered arm and arm.

A time of laughter, tears, and blessing can draw you closer together as a family and affirm the love you have shared over the years.

> *My heart is overflowing with a good theme;*
> *I recite my composition . . .*
> *My tongue is the pen of a ready writer.*
> —PS. 45:1

Don't forget how an everyday object used as a word picture can bring encouragement to your parents' hearts.

One person told her mother, "Mom, when we were growing up, you reminded me of a fork. Your eyes were always sharp enough to catch us when we were doing something wrong, and you had more than one good point!"

Sure, it's corny, but it communicates. We're sure at least twenty objects in the very room in which you sit could stimulate your thoughts and give you a "good theme" for pointing out the high value of your parents.

Use your quiet time today to write a word picture revealing what your parents mean to you. (It would make a wonderful Christmas gift!)

She answered, "Give me a blessing."
—JOSH. 15:19

Today's scripture is a request for real estate, but it also is a daughter's (Achsah's) straightforward request for her father's (Caleb's) blessing. Asking for a blessing can be one of the most meaningful ways we can honor our parents! Lee Ezell tells of when such a request helped heal a serious breach in her husband's family:

> Years ago Hal and his father experienced a theological separation.... Basically, the elder Ezell was right, but Hal didn't know it at the time. After a number of years my husband began to try to heal the breach. One Sunday he went to his father and said, "Dad, I would like your blessing." Dad has been a pastor for decades, and in the very same way he had blessed thousands of churchgoers before, he very soberly laid his hands on Hal's head and prayed for God's blessing. He showed no emotion. He shed no tears. But his gesture touched Hal and me deeply, and in a very real way.*

What better way to communicate to our parents that they are "heavy-weights" in our life than by asking for their blessing?

*Lee Ezell, *Pills for Parents in Pain* (Dallas: Word, 1992), ch. 10.

For You have formed my inward parts; You have covered me in my mother's womb. I will praise You, for I am fearfully and wonderfully made.
—PS. 139:13–14

If you are one of those people who have difficulty blessing your parents, a good place to start might be with the basic fact of your existence. No matter what your parents have done, you still owe them honor for being the vessels by which God brought you into the world. In a sense, to dishonor them is to dishonor your existence.

But that's just the problem for a lot of us, isn't it? Our experiences in growing up have led us to curse ourselves—to esteem ourselves lightly. In order to bless our parents or anyone else, we need a strong reminder from Scripture of just how important we are to God. Important enough for Him to form our inward parts. Important enough to watch over and protect. Important enough to come to earth and share our human plight. Important enough to die for. With that vote of confidence, who are we to contradict Him?

As you celebrate Christ's coming into the world, bless your parents for being the means by which you—a very special person loved by Him—came into the world.

For God so loved the world that He gave His only begotten Son, that whoever believes in Him should not perish but have everlasting life. —JOHN 3:16

Left on our own, we human beings inevitably taint our blessings. Call it selfishness, human fallibility, sin—whatever you call it, we have this maddening tendency to foul up every good thing we get our hands on. Even love. Even parenthood. Even blessings. Even Christmas. The awful, but honest, truth is that left on our own, we humans have always made a mess of our earth and the creatures who populate it.

But the wonderful news of the gospel is that God has never left us on our own! Over the centuries, while we have rebelled, hidden, and hurt each other, God has persistently loved us, showing us how to get His blessing and how to bless others. Finally, when we persisted in our stubborn sin, God gave the ultimate gift—the gift of His Son. Because of this, all our yearnings for a blessing can be satisfied. All our flawed efforts at blessing others can be redeemed. Christmas happens in spite of everything. And everything will be all right!

On this day of gifts, meditate on the gift that has made all our blessings possible.

> *And all these blessings shall come upon you and*
> *overtake you, because you obey the voice of the*
> *LORD your God.*
> —DEUT. 28:2

Sometimes the harder you try to get something, the more it eludes you. A teenager is desperate to have a steady, but never gets a date. The writer who wants to start the "Great American Novel" stares at a blank computer screen for hours. Many dynamics could be at work in these frustrating situations. But surely one problem is confusing a realistic goal with a wonderful by-product. A realistic purpose in dating is getting to know people of the opposite sex. Getting a steady is a by-product. The realistic purpose of sitting at the computer is to tell a story or communicate a message. Producing a classic or a best-seller is a by-product.

The blessing is a by-product, too. We are called to love God and obey Him, not to go out and get blessed. But the difference between being blessed and those other sometimes frustrating pursuits is that God's blessing is a *guaranteed* by-product.

If we obey God's voice (and part of that obedience is blessing others),
we will receive all the blessings He has promised to us.

Render therefore to all their due: taxes to whom taxes are due, customs to whom customs, fear to whom fear, honor to whom honor. —ROM. 13:7

Being a person of blessing means always looking for people we can bless. But if we stay open to the Holy Spirit's prompting, we may find ourselves giving the elements to a variety of people:

- the big brothers who always beat up on you (or the little sister who always told on you)
- the neighbor whose dog barks all night
- your boss
- your mother-in-law
- the grocery store checkout clerk
- your child's third-grade teacher

Clearly, the blessing you give to a store clerk will be different from the blessing you give to your mother-in-law—the level of your acquaintance is different. But once you start looking, you will find that the opportunities to "be a blessing" are almost limitless.

Commit yourself to trying to bless all the people whose lives touch yours.

Do as the occasion demands; for God is with you.
—1 SAM. 10:7

Today's verse contains Samuel's instructions to Saul after anointing him to be king, but his advice is also a reminder to take advantage of occasions to give the blessing. Any day is a good day to bless someone, but some days are especially rich in "blessing opportunities." Birthdays, baptisms, confirmations, and weddings are natural possibilities. A little creative thought will uncover other great opportunities to provide special blessings.

Getting a driver's license, for instance, is a major rite of passage. You could hand over the car keys with a few well-chosen words that affirm your love and trust. (This particular blessing may require more than a little faith on your part!) The first day of a new job also presents a wonderful opportunity for you to love and affirm a spouse or friend with a few words of blessing—or send flowers with a loving note. How about a blessing for your son's first date, your kindergartner's first day of school, a friend's first night in a new house? Once you start blessing others, you'll find a million occasions on which to do so!

Write your own list of special days that offer you an opportunity to give a blessing.

Go, eat your bread with joy. . . .
for God has already accepted your works.
—ECCL. 9:7

Here are some final ideas we've heard for giving the "daily bread" of blessing:

1. We used a special red plate at dinner to designate birthdays or outstanding achievements.
2. Every Saturday morning, my father would get up first and cook us all pancakes and bacon.
3. Our family always went out to eat after church and discussed what we had learned at Sunday school.
4. My father would ask to talk to each of us kids personally when he called home from a trip.
5. We would hold hands when we said grace; then when we finished, we would squeeze the person's hand next to us three times, which stood for the three words, "I love you."
6. My mother would slow down when I helped her cook to let us accomplish the task together.
7. I had never seen him cry before, but my father cried during my wedding because he was going to miss my not being at home.

Today, review your original statement of dreams and expectations for the year. Reflect and rejoice in the realization that your efforts at blessing are already accepted and approved!

So you may walk in the way of goodness.
—PROV. 2:20

Here is a New Year's blessing based on Proverbs 2:1–8. Give it to someone you love:

My [son or daughter or husband or wife—or whatever!], if you will:

- Receive and believe what God says . . .
- Treasure with high value His commandments . . .
- Listen attentively to His wisdom . . .
- Draw your heart to understand Him . . .
- Cry for discernment . . .
- Raise your voice for understanding . . .
- Seek Him more than silver or hidden treasures . . .

You will understand how to honor God. God will give you knowledge and wisdom. From Him you will receive understanding, for God has stored up wisdom for you because you have sought Him above all else. He will be your shield and your bodyguard. He will preserve your way.

Begin your New Year with a blessing for the people you love. Help them "walk in the way of goodness."

The LORD bless you and keep you;
the LORD make His face to shine upon you,
and be gracious to you;
the LORD lift up His countenance upon you,
and give you peace."   —NUM. 6:24–26

As we end the year and this devotional book, we hope you've been encouraged and challenged to be a person of blessing. But we don't want to leave you with just our thoughts on these pages. We would also like to leave you with our blessing for you. If we could reach out to each of you reading this book and place our hands on your shoulders, our final blessing would be the words of today's scripture—a blessing that has been a source of joy and encouragement to Christians over the centuries.

Our prayer is that God will enable you to become a mighty source of blessing, and that these words will always ring true in your life.

We wish you abundant blessings for yourself and those you love throughout the New Year.

About the Authors

Gary Smalley, president of Today's Family, is a doctoral candidate in marriage and family counseling and has a master's degree from Bethel Seminary in St. Paul, Minnesota. His previous best-selling books include *If Only He Knew, For Better or for Best, Joy That Lasts,* and *The Key to Your Child's Heart.* He and his wife, Norma, are the parents of three children, Kari, Greg, and Michael.

John Trent, vice president of Today's Family, has a Ph.D. in marriage and family counseling and holds a master's degree from Dallas Theological Seminary. He wrote with Gary the best-selling books, *The Blessing, The Gift of Honor, The Language of Love, Love Is a Decision,* and *The Two Sides of Love.* He lives in Phoenix with his wife, Cynthia, and daughters, Kari Lorraine and Laura Catherine.